Revise for Edexcel GCSE Textiles Technolog

Sue Manser

Series Editor: Chris Weaving

Success through qualifications

Heinemann Educational Publishers
Halley Court, Jordan Hill, Oxford OX2 8EJ
Part of Harcourt Education Limited

Heinemann is a registered trademark of
Harcourt Education Limited

Text © Sue Manser and Chris Weaving, 2003

First published 2003
06 05 04 03
10 9 8 7 6 5 4 3 2 1

British Library Cataloguing in Publication Data
A catalogue record for this book is available from the British Library on request.

ISBN 0 435 41718 5

Typeset by Tech-Set Ltd
Printed in the UK by Bath Press Ltd

Original illustrations © Harcourt Education Limited, 2002
Illustrated by Hardlines and Tech-Set Ltd

Cover photographs by: ImageBank (shoe), Images Colour Library (material on rollers), John Walmsley (students pinning clothes).

Acknowledgements
Every effort has been made to contact copyright holders of material reproduced in this book. Any omissions will be rectified in subsequent printings if notice is given to the publishers.

Brother p. 58; Linda Straw p. 38; Science Photo Library/Deep Light Productions p. 45; Science Photo Library/ Philippe Plailly p. 59; Sophis p. 38; Speed Step p. 54 (all)

Tel: 01865 888058 www.heinemann.co.uk

CONTENTS

If yes read on …

What is revision?

Revision in preparation for an examination is defined as *reviewing previously learned material.*

Why revise?

The purpose of revision is to:
- *refresh your knowledge and understanding* of previously learned material;
- *improve your ability to recall and apply this knowledge and understanding* to the questions on the examination paper.

How can revision improve my grade?

The written examination paper:
- is worth 40% of the whole examination (the other 60% comes from coursework);
- has four questions, each worth 10% of the whole examination.

Therefore, thorough revision that enables four questions to be answered well, can earn a large proportion of these marks and contribute significantly to the final grade awarded.

Do I need to know about all the content listed in the Exam Board Specification?

Yes because:
- the examination board will test all content listed in the Specification at least once during its life (normally five years);
- if something has been tested once, it does not mean it will not be tested again in a future exam paper.

It is therefore essential that you prepare fully by revising everything listed in the Specification.

How does this book help me?

It has been written by examiners who know:
- how the questions are written;
- what is needed in the answers.

What does the book tell me?

The book contains important information about the examination paper and about what you need to know.

1 Section 1 tells you about the examination paper:
   - how it is structured;
   - how to manage your time answering the questions;
   - how part questions are structured;
   - how to write your answers to access all of the marks.
   - the importance of *Key Words* in each part question;
2 Section 2 and Section 3:
   - combine some content headings from the Examination Board Specification to form single *Topic* headings;
   - show how these content headings must be integrated when applied to designing;
   - help you to understand how to apply the knowledge and understanding you already have, to designing;
   - help you focus your revision and make more effective use of that time.
3 Section 4 helps you to:
   - understand the *Design Question* (not Short Course);
   - understand the *Product Analysis Question*.
   - recognise the types of part questions that may be included;
   - recognise what is needed to answer each question successfully by giving sample answers.

Do the *Topics* tell me what I need to know to answer the exam questions?

Yes. These *Topics*:

- are introduced by identifying the major areas of the Specification content for which you need to have an appropriate level of knowledge and understanding;
- expand this content into *Key Points*.

What do the *Key Points* tell me?

The *Key Points*:

- identify the detail of what you need to know;
- focus the detail towards its application in product design and make/manufacture i.e. how different materials properties present design opportunities and how different making/manufacturing processes present design opportunities.

What about industrial applications?

The industrial applications icon will show where industrial processes are addressed within each *Topic*.

Are there any sample questions and answers?

Yes. Each *Topic* will include sample part questions, complete with full answers to show:

- how questions might be asked;
- the depth and breadth of knowledge and understanding required;
- how to present answers to access all of the marks.

The examination board will test all content listed in the Specification at least once during its life (normally five years). However, just because a topic has been tested once, does not mean it will not be tested again. It is therefore essential that you prepare fully by revising all topics listed in the Specification.

 This icon indicates an Industrial Application

 This icon indicates information not required for the Short Course

Section 1
Revision strategy
and explanation

THE QUESTION PAPER

Short course (SC)

There will be two different question papers, one each for the foundation and higher tiers. For the examination you will be given one of these papers.

The question paper will be marked out of a total of 44 marks.

The time for answering the paper is 1 hour.

All questions are compulsory and must be answered in the spaces provided on the question paper.

Each question paper will have three separate questions as follows:

- Two questions will test specific knowledge and understanding from AO1* and will be worth 11 marks each (see further guidance in this section and Section 2).

- One question will test product analysis AO3* (iii) and will be worth 22 marks (see Sections 3 and 4).

* AO1 and AO3 are the Assessment Objectives listed in Edexcel's Subject Specification booklet. They contain the knowledge and understanding that the examination questions will be based upon. Section 2 of this book deals with AO1 and Section 3 deals with AO3.

Examiner's Tip

To score as many marks as you are able, you must attempt all questions and part questions.

Full course (FC)

There will be two different question papers, one each for the foundation and higher tiers. For the examination you will be given one of these papers.

The question paper will be marked out of a total of 88 marks.

The time for answering the paper is $1\frac{1}{2}$ hours.

All questions are compulsory and must be answered in the spaces provided on the question paper.

Each question paper will have four separate questions as follows:

- One question, 22 marks, will test specific knowledge and understanding from AO1* (see further guidance in this section and Section 2).

- The first half of another question, 11 marks, will test different specific knowledge and understanding from AO1*, with the second half testing specific knowledge and understanding from AO3* (i) and (ii), 11 marks (see further guidance in this section and Sections 2 and 3).

- The design question, 22 marks, will test AO2* (see Section 4).
- The product analysis question, 22 marks, will test AO3 (iii) (see Section 4).

* AO1, AO2 and AO3 are the Assessment Objectives listed in Edexcel's Subject Specification booklet. AO1 and AO3 contain the knowledge and understanding that the examination questions will be based upon. Section 2 of this book deals with AO1 and Section 3 deals with AO3.

xaminer's Tip

To score as many marks as you are able, you must attempt all questions and part questions.

Short course and full course (SC/FC)
Each separate question will be divided into smaller part questions labelled (a), (b), (c), etc. These part questions are likely to be progressively more difficult.

Alphabetically labelled part questions, for example (a), may also be divided further into smaller parts and these are labelled, (i), (ii), (iii), etc. These smaller parts will all be linked to the common theme of this part question.

The marks available for each part question are shown at the end of that part question for example **(2 marks)**.

xaminer's Tip

These marks also suggest how long you should spend answering each question. For example, you should spend approximately twice as long thinking about and answering a question worth 2 marks compared to answering a question worth 1 mark.

On all question papers the potentially easier questions will be towards the beginning of the paper, with those that are potentially more difficult towards the end. This also applies to the part questions within a whole question, that is, there is an increase in difficulty between the beginning and end of the paper and between the beginning and end of each question.

xaminer's Tip

Make sure each answer fully satisfies the question set. That is, if you give simple one-word answers to the more valuable questions, you will not score many marks.

How you should answer individual questions

Each part question will use a key word to tell you the type of answer that is required. Some key words and answer types are as follows:

Key words	Answer type
Give State Name	Normally a one- or two-word answer, at the very most a short sentence.
Name the specific	As above, but requires specific detail to be given. Generic answers such as 'cotton' or 'wool' will gain no marks.
Describe	Normally, one or two sentences which form a description, making reference to more than one point. All points must be linked for a complete answer.
Explain	Normally, one or two sentences which form an explanation. This requires a clear or detailed account of something and includes a relevant justification, reason or example.
Use notes and sketches Annotated sketches	Mainly a sketched answer with notes to support or clarify particular points in the answer. 'Sketch' means 'a quick freehand drawing'. Marks are awarded for the technical accuracy of the information communicated in the answer rather than the drawing skills shown.
Evaluate	Normally one or two sentences where the quality, suitability or value of something is judged. This can include both positive and negative points, with each point normally requiring a relevant justification, reason or example.

Examiner's Tip

The number of pieces of information required in any answer will be shown by the number of marks given to the part question.

Examiner's Tip

The space given on the question paper suggests the maximum that you should write or draw in answer to any question.

Examiner's Tip

No marks are given for repeating information given in the question.

Examiner's Tip

Where / is used in an example answer, it means that what follows is an alternative to the part of the answer that precedes it, not an addition.

The following example questions and answers illustrate the use of the main key words in part questions and the different style and length of answers required.

Q1 *A manufacturer is making a clutch bag from cotton calico fabric.*

   (i) *Name **two** different methods of colouring cotton calico fabric.*

1 ....

2 ....

                                                     (2 marks)

A full answer requires two different colouring methods to be named. For example:

1 Screen printing.

2 Resist dye.

Q2   **(i)** *Describe **one** quality of weft knitted fabrics that make them suitable for clothing products.*

....

....

                                                     (2 marks)

A full answer for 2 marks requires a statement containing two linked points. For example:

Weft knitted fabrics have an ability to stretch and still regain their shape.

Q3 *Many people use swimming as a regular form of exercise and relaxation.*

   (i) *Explain **two** reasons why manufacturers now use elastane fibres to produce swimwear.*

1 ....

....

2 ....

....

                                                     (4 marks)

A full answer for 4 marks requires two different reasons to be identified and the importance of each to be explained or justified. For example:

1 Elastane fibres make fabrics that dry easily because they are lightweight.

2 Swimwear made from elastane can improve performance because it fits so firmly and closely.

 xaminer's Tip

Note that both of these answers have two parts to them, each linked by the word 'because'.

Section 2
Assessment
Objective 1

You need to know that:

☐ Primary fibres are either natural or manufactured.

☐ Primary processing carried out on fibres converts them into yarns.

☐ Yarns are further processed into fabrics.

PRIMARY FIBRES

Primary fibres are either natural or manufactured fibres.

- Natural fibres are either animal, i.e. wool and silk, or vegetable, i.e. cotton or linen (these are cellulose fibres).

- Manufactured fibres are either cellulosic (regenerated or man made), i.e. viscose, acetate, Tencel, or synthetic, i.e. mircofibres, acrylic, polyester, polyamide (nylon), elastane (Lycra) or aramid (Kevlar). Nylon, Lycra and Kevlar are trade names.

PRIMARY PROCESSING

Primary processing of fibres creates yarns.

- Fibres can be short and spun into a yarn.

- Longer fibres are called filament yarns, e.g. silk and polyester and these are spun into yarn.

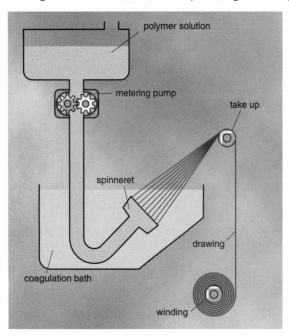

Wet spinning

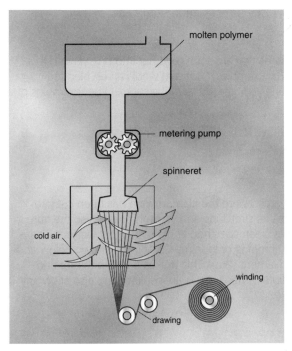

Melt spinning

Every spun yarn has either a Z twist or an S twist which has an effect on the yarn's appearance.

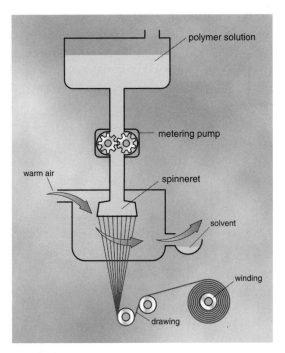

Dry spinning

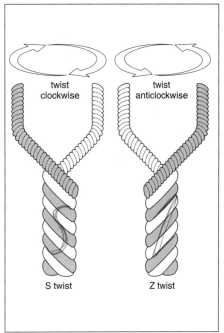

S twist and Z twist of fibres

→ The twist effects the lustre and shine of the fabric.

Several yarns can be spun together, i.e. two yarns spun together create two-ply yarns; three yarns spun together create three-ply yarns.

Yarn blends or blended yarns are two fibres that are spun together into one yarn so that the qualities of the yarn can be improved. For example, nylon and wool can be blended together to improve strength and the resulting yarn is used to make socks. Other examples of blending yarns are:

- polyester and cotton to improve performance properties e.g. elasticity;
- cotton and viscose to make the yarn more economical;
- multi-colour to make a decorative effect.

Textured or bulked fibres are synthetic yarns where the filament yarn has been cut into shorter lengths before spinning. This reduces its stretching and warmth qualities so the fibre is 'bulked' to help the fibre recover when it has been stretched and also make it warmer. This is done in several different ways, i.e. twisting; crimping or looping. Crimping is shown below and is achieved by blowing a jet of air over the filament yarns. This makes the yarn thicker and softer and creates air spaces between the fibres. These act as an insulator and also allow any fabric made from the yarn to 'breathe'.

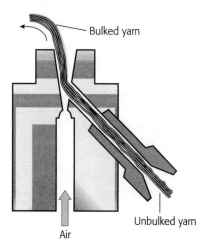

Tactel fibres crimped by air bulking

Examination questions

Q1 *Give the specific names of **two** natural fibres used in textile products.*

1 ....

2 ....

Acceptable answer
Any two from:
- Wool
- Silk
- Cotton
- Linen.

Examiner's Tip

The question asks for **specific** names therefore general names such as animal fibres or vegetable fibres will not score any marks.

Q2 *Elastane is a synthetic manufactured fibre.*

i) *Give **one** trade name used to identify this fibre when used in textile products.*

Acceptable answer
Any one from:
- Lycra
- Spandex.

Examiner's Tip

The question gives a generic name, Elastane, for the fibre. Different manufacturers produce this fibre and each registers it under their own **trade name**. It is an example of the trade name that is required as the answer to this question.

ii) *Name **two** regenerated manufactured fibres.*

1 ....

2 ....

2 marks

Acceptable answer

Any two from:
Generic names:
- Viscose
- Acetate
- Triacetate
- Lyocell.

OR

Trade names:
- Dicel
- Tricel
- Tencel

Or any **one** of the following:
- Rayon Fibro
- Evlan
- Sarille

Examiner's Tip

The question requires two different regenerated fibres to be named, therefore be careful not to give a generic name as one answer and the trade name for the same fibre as your second answer, e.g. Viscose and Rayon, as this will only score one mark.

Q3 *Nylon is blended with wool to produce a yarn used to make socks. Explain **one** reason why this blended yarn is better suited for making socks than a yarn made from pure wool.*

2 marks

....

....

Acceptable answer

Nylon fibre is stronger than woollen fibre therefore the yarn produced from blending the two **is stronger than one produced from pure wool/will last longer than one produced from pure wool**.

Q4 *Crimping is one method used for bulking filament yarn. Describe **one** improvement to the working characteristics of filament yarn that results from crimping.*

2 marks

....

....

Acceptable answer

Any one of the following:
- crimping makes the yarn **thicker** and **softer**;
- crimping makes **air spaces between the fibres** which **act as an insulator**/which **allows any fabric made from the yarn to 'breathe' more easily**.

You need to know that:

☐ Yarns are made into fabrics in different ways.

    ☐ Woven fabric

    ☐ Non-woven

    ☐ Knitted

    ☐ Woven, non-woven and knitted fabrics have different structural properties.

WOVEN FABRIC

Woven fabrics do not stretch as much as knitted fabrics. They have yarns running across the width and down the length of the fabric. The threads that run the length of the fabric are called 'warp threads' those that run across the fabric are called 'weft threads'.

xaminer's Tip

Weft goes left to right and right to left, e.g. the threads run across the width of the fabric.

Woven fabric is constructed on both hand and machine looms. The weft threads are used to create different structures or weaves. Plain and twill weave are the most common. Looms are computerised and can produce fabric in a variety of widths.

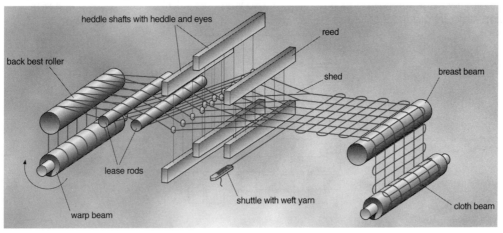

How a weaving loom works

INDUSTRIAL APPLICATION

The width of the fabric is directly related to the width of the loom. Standard widths for fabrics are 90 cm, 115 cm and 140 cm. Occasionally fabrics are 150 cm wide but these are usually used for soft furnishing. The edge of woven fabric is called the selvedge.

Designs can be woven into fabrics and effects can be achieved by using different threads for the warp and the weft.

Plain weave is produced by passing a weft thread under and over the warp threads alternatively, creating a firm structure.

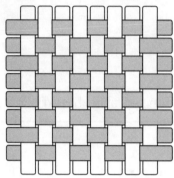

Plain weave

Plain weaving can be used to produce calico, gingham and poplin fabrics.

- **Calico** is a very cheap fabric used in the fashion industry to produce a prototype or toile. This allows the designer to see and adjust the finished product. It is soft and creases easily as it has no finishes added to it. Calico is also used for tye-dyeing.
- **Gingham** is a thin checked fabric. The checks are produced by setting up the warp threads in different blocks of colours. The weft threads are also used in blocks of colours to produce the checked effect. Gingham is often used to make school summer dresses, lightweight summer shirts and blouses.
- **Poplin** is a firmer plain woven fabric which is usually plain in colour. It is used to make garments that need to 'hold their shape' for example jackets, trousers, skirts and tailored dresses.

Passing two weft threads under and over the two warp threads alternatively creating a very firm structure produces twill weave.

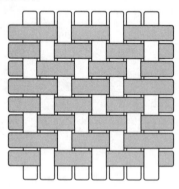

Twill weave

- **Denim** is used to make garments and items that need to withstand 'wear and tear'. It is a very firm fabric. It has a blue warp thread and a white weft thread. The weaving increases the durability of the fabric. Denim is used to make jeans, jackets, skirts, dungarees, shorts and many accessories especially bags.

- **Herringbone** is a twill weave which changes sequence regularly to produce a pattern on the surface of the fabric. Herringbone weave can be produced in one or two colours. Herringbone weave is a firm fabric, which gives structure to the products it is used to produce. It is often used for coats, suits and jackets.

Herringbone weave

NON-WOVEN FABRICS

Non-woven fabric is divided into two groups; felt fabrics and bonded fibre fabrics. They are both produced from a tangle of fibres, which are flattened and joined together.

Felt fabrics are traditionally made from woollen fibres which matt together when heated because the scales on the fibres become tangled together. Felt is now also made from synthetic or recycled yarns. Felt is used for creative work, for example soft toy making, it can be steamed into shape and used to make hats and is used as covering on snooker and pool tables.

Bonded fibre fabrics are made from a web of fibres which are randomly distributed and then bonded together using one of the following; fabric adhesive, heat or solvents to soften the fibres. These fabrics are used for a variety of products including head restraint covers on aircraft, train and coach seats and disposable products such as aprons, cleaning cloths, hospital gowns, sheets and underwear.

Vilene® is a bonded fibre fabric. It is used for interfacings and interlinings to strengthen other fabrics during their construction into textile products. Vilene® can be in 'sew-in' or in a fusible 'iron-on' form. It can be used in collars, cuffs, waistbands of skirts and trousers and the fronts of shirts and blouses under the buttonholes. Vilene® is economical to produce and creates little waste in use.

Properties of non-woven fabrics.
- They are inexpensive to make because the fibres do not have to be made into yarns.
- They do not fray when cut because they have no 'grain'.
- They are good insulators because they have lots of air spaces between their fibres.
- They do not hang well because they are rather stiff.
- They are not elastic and distort when stretched.

KNITTED FABRICS

Fabrics that are knitted are constructed in two ways; either weft knitting or warp knitting.
- Weft knitted fabrics are knitted across the fabric and can ladder very easily.
- Warp knitted fabrics are knitted vertically, interlocking different chains of knitting. The fabric is firm and does not ladder.

Knitted fabrics can be produced by hand or by machine. Machine knitting can be done on small 'home' knitting machines or large industrial machines. Knitted products are often warm as they trap air between the stitches and this helps to insulate the wearer.

Hand knitting can be produced using either plain or purl stitch, and uses the weft method (across the fabric). Wool, acrylic, cotton or a synthetic mix are usually used for hand knitting. The thickness of the knitting depends on the ply of the knitting yarn and the size of the knitting needles used.

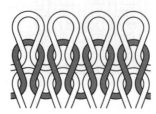

Weft knitting

Hand knitting can be used to produce jumpers, cardigans, socks, scarves, hats and gloves. Knitting will stretch, e.g. over the head or hands but it will regain its shape. Hand knitting can 'sag' but regains its stretch and shape when washed.

Machine knitting produces items using the warp or weft method. Weft knitting is more elastic, having a high level of stretch, but it will ladder. It is used to make swim wear, aerobic clothing, underwear, socks and tights.

Single Jersey is a finely knitted fabric. Hand knitters call this stocking stitch. It will not ladder. It drapes well and is comfortable to wear. Jersey can be produced with both natural and synthetic fibres. Polyester jersey is used to make dresses and skirts; cotton jersey is used to make tee shirts.

Double jersey is made on a 'double bed machine' that uses two sets of needles, each with its own supply of yarn. This means that the fabric is much thicker and firmer than single jersey. It has much less stretch than single jersey. It is used to make jackets, dresses, skirts and coats.

Warp knitted polyester fleece is made from recycled plastic bottles. It is slightly stretchy and keeps its shape well. It is a good insulator. The fabric has a loop created during the knitting process. Polyester fleece can be used to make training tops, jumpers, sweatshirts and children's play clothes.

Warp knitting

Examination questions

Q1 *Look at the diagram of a piece of fabric below.*

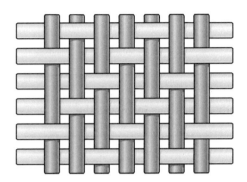

i) *Name the weave used to construct the fabric.*

....

ii) *On the diagram label the following*
- *The selvedge edge*
- *The warp threads*
- *The weft threads*

Acceptable answer

i) Twill weave

ii)

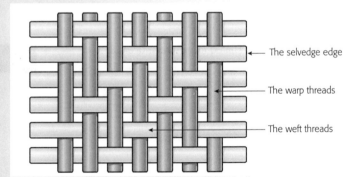

— The selvedge edge

— The warp threads

— The weft threads

xaminer's Tip

Answers must be specific, i.e. twill weave is the only acceptable answer. Marks would not be gained by giving an answer such as weave for jeans or denim weave.

xaminer's Tip

When labelling diagrams, ensure that you indicate exactly the place that the answer refers to.

Q2 Explain **one** reason why twill weave is often used for constructing jeans.

2 marks

....

....

Acceptable answer

The weave creates **diagonal strength** and therefore **increases the durability** of the fabric.

Q3 Knitted fabric is widely used in today's clothing market.

i) Describe **two** qualities of plain fabrics that make them suitable for clothing products

4 marks

....

....

....

....

ii) Explain **one** advantage that warp knitted fabrics have over weft knitted fabrics.

2 marks

....

....

....

....

iii) Give **one** way in which the direction of twist of the yarn influences the appearance of the fabric.

....

....

Acceptable answer

i) Knitted fabrics **stretch and spring back to shape**, and are suitable for clothing which needs **to 'hug' the body**, e.g. tights, underwear, gloves and hats.

Knitted fabrics have **small holes which trap air** and **act as an insulator**.

ii) Warp knitting is **interlocked on the diagonal** therefore it **does not ladder** like weft knitting.

iii) The twist of the yarn will affect the **lustre or shine** of the finished fabric.

Examiner's Tip

Be careful not to state that smalll holes trap **heat** – which they do not.

Q4 Name **two** non-woven fabrics.

2 marks

1 ....

2 ....

Acceptable answer

Felt
Vilene

Q5 Non-woven fabrics can be constructed by bondng fibres together.

Give **three** stages of constructing a bonded fabric.

3 marks

1 ....

2 ....

3 ....

Acceptable answer

1 The fibres are laid down in a random web.
2 The fibres are glued together.
3. Heat is applied to set the glue.

Q6 Gingham is a fabric often used for school summer shirts or dresses.
Give **three** properties that make this fabric suitable for these shirts and give **one** reason for **each**.

Property 1 ....

Reason ....

Property 2 ....

Reason ....

Property 3 ....

Reason ....

Acceptable answer

Property 1	Washable
Reason	School shirts **get dirty** quickly
Property 2	Cool to wear
Reason	Gingham is **absorbent**
Property 3	Easy to care
Reason	Needs **little ironing**

Q7 Describe **two different** points that must be considered when cuttting pattern pieces from gingham fabric to ensure a quality finish.

1 ....

2 ....

Acceptable answer

1 The fabric must be **cut on the straight grain** to ensure the **checks are parallel**.

2 The **checks must match** when the **garment is constructed**/Gingham **has a nap** which must be **taken into account when cutting the fabric**.

xaminer's Tip

Nap refers to a one-way pattern or checks. It is a technical term, which you are encouraged to use. Be careful to use two different answers to this question and not repeat the same answer in another way. You will only gain full marks for two different points.

Q8 Cotton is a natural fibre, which can be used for a wide range of products. One advantage is that cotton is hardwearing

Give **two** other advantages of using cotton fibre fabrics and explain your answer.

Advantage 1 ....

....

Advantage 2 ....

....

Acceptable answer

Advantage 1 Cotton is **absorbent** and therefore suitable for **clothing worn next to the skin/household items such as towels and tea-towels**.

Advantage 2 Cotton is **strong and hardwearing** therefore it can be used for **work clothing/items that need constant cleaning**.

Q9 Describe **one** way in which cotton fabric can be made warmer to wear.

....

....

Acceptable answer

Cotton can **be knitted** which means **air can be trapped** within the fabric.

Q10 Describe how a 'toile' is used in industrial manufacture.

....

....

Acceptable answer

It allows the designer to **check the quality of design and cut before full-scale production**.

Fabric performance

You need to know that:

☐ The functional properties of the original fibre fabric affect fabric performance.

☐ The aesthetic properties of the original fibre fabric affect fabric performance.

☐ Individual fabrics can have several natural properties and can have these changed by chemical processes.

FUNCTIONAL PROPERTIES

Functional properties are **absorbency, easy-care, durability, elasticity, flammability, strength, thermoplastic, warmth, waterproof, breathability, windproof** and **stain resistance**. Each fibre has its own individual functional properties; these determine how a fibre will behave during use.

- Absorbency – how much moisture will the fabric absorb?
- Easy-care – does the fabric wash and iron easily?
- Durability – is the fabric able to withstand wear and tear? Does it withstand abrasion?
- Elasticity – will the fabric return to its original shape easily?
- Flammability – does the fabric burn easily and what happens when it does burn?
- Strength – is the fibre/fabric strong when wet?
- Thermoplastic – fibres that can be softened by heat and set while cooling, e.g. permanent pleating.
- Warmth – is the fabric a good insulator and will it keep the wearer warm?
- Waterproof – does the fabric repel water, e.g. does a water droplet remain on the surface of the fabric?
- Breathability – does the fabric allow the wearer's body to breathe?
- Windproof – does the fabric construction help it to withstand wind?
- Stain resistance – will the fabric stain easily or will it resist stains?

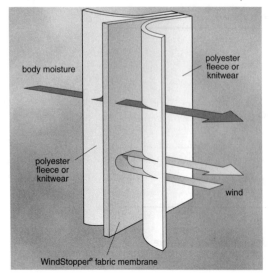

How Gore-tex WindStopper® fabric works

AESTHETIC PROPERTIES

Aesthetic properties **are colour, texture, handle, drape, softness, lustre, weight, crease-resistance,** and **fineness**.

- Handle – is the fabric easy to work with or does it fray?
- Drape – how the fabric hangs; is it firm and therefore stiff when it drapes?
- Softness – does the fabric feel soft to the skin?
- Lustre – does the fibre/fabric have a natural shine or sheen?
- Weight – how heavy or light is the fabric? This is determined by the ply of the yarn and the weaving or knitting technique employed during production.
- Crease-resistance – how easily does a fabric crease? Will this effect the wearing of the garment? Does a crease-resistant finish need applying to the fabric?
- Fineness – how fine is the yarn and therefore the constructed fabric?

Individual fabrics can have several properties naturally and can have these changed by chemical means.

PROPERTIES OF NATURAL FIBRE FABRICS

Cotton

- Cotton is able to absorb moisture up to 40 per cent of its own weight. The absorbed moisture evaporates quickly so this makes cotton cool to wear. If left damp in a heap cotton will be attacked by mildew.
- It is a strong fibre, which becomes stronger when wet. It therefore resists abrasion and is durable.
- It is not harmed by alkalis, heat or bleach if used with care.
- Cotton fibres can be brushed or treated to make them fluffy therefore making them warmer because they will then trap air.

Because cotton is strong and hard wearing it can be blended with other fibres to reduce costs and improve the wearing qualities.

The aesthetic properties of cotton can be changed using physical finishes. These are applied to the fabric after it has been constructed.

- Calendaring is the technical name for the process that gives a shine to the surface of the fabric; it is only used on cotton fabrics. The fabric is pressed between two rollers and the friction causes the polishing.
- Brushing is used to give the fabric a hairy surface so air becomes trapped in the surface and makes the fabric warmer. Cotton is brushed to make winceyette or flannelette; both are warm and absorbent.

Chemical finishes can also be added to fabrics, which will change their natural properties. They can be applied during yarn construction, during fabric construction or after fabric construction.

- Bleaching is a chemical finish which changes the colour of the fibre or fabric, making it easier to dye and/or apply other colours. Some fabrics are bleached to create a finished effect, e.g. denim.
- Easy-care finish is applied to cotton fabrics as they crease easily. This is applied to help with the washing and ironing process. The textile product dries well and needs little ironing. It is often used on shirts and blouses.

- Mercerising is applied to cotton fibre or fabric to give sheen. Cotton poplin is often mercerised to improve its appearance.
- Laminating is a plastic coating which is chemically applied to fabric to ensure that it is waterproof. This can be used for items such as aprons and table covers and it is often cotton that is laminated.

Linen

- Linen is stronger than cotton but is not at all elastic. This makes it suitable for industrial application where it is important that the fabric does not stretch, e.g. hose pipes and soft furnishings.
- The fibres will split or break if treated badly during laundering. If folds are ironed continually in the same place the fibres will crack.
- It creases easily but can be treated with a crease resistant finish.
- It absorbs more moisture than cotton making it suitable for clothes worn in hot climates. The moisture evaporates quickly making it cool to wear. If left damp for any length of time linen will be attacked by mildew.
- The fibres are very smooth giving them a natural sheen.
- It is very durable.
- It is the most difficult natural fibre to dye.

Because linen is difficult to dye it is often bleached before a colour is added. This allows linen products to be made in a range of colours. An easy-care finish is also commonly applied to linen fabrics as they crease very easily. It is often used on men and women's suits.

Wool

- Wool has a high level of elasticity. This makes the fabrics, which are woven or knitted from wool, very elastic or stretchy. Because wool stretches it 'gives' or moves with the body.
- When washed wool products regain their shape.
- It is very absorbent and can take up to 30 per cent of its own weight in moisture before feeling damp. As it absorbs the water vapour the wool gains extra warmth; this makes it ideal for winter clothing as the body moisture is absorbed and the trapped air gives off warmth.
- It is also water repellent. A droplet of water on a wool fabric will stand for some time before being absorbed.
- It gives warmth and is a good insulator because the overlapping scales trap heat in pockets of air.

Silk

- Silk is a good insulator, warm to wear in the winter and cool in the summer.
- It is absorbent and is slightly warmer when damp, but perspiration will rot silk fabric.
- It is the strongest natural fibre.
- It is very elastic which makes it wear well. The elastic quality makes it crease resistant.
- It has a soft sheen and it drapes well.
- It can be lightweight or weighted to make it suitable for furnishing fabrics.
- Mild acids do not harm silk; the natural colour of silk is difficult to bleach to pure white.

PROPERTIES OF MANUFACTURED FIBRE FABRICS

Viscose
- Viscose absorbs moisture and is a good conductor of heat.
- It is mothproof and is not subject to mildew.
- It can be blended or mixed with wool.
- It is weaker when wet and should not be twisted when washed.
- It drapes well and is soft to handle.
- Colour is added to the spinning solution therefore it does not require dyeing.
- It burns very easily and needs to have a chemical finish applied to it. Flame resist is a durable finish that can be damaged by washing powders.

Acetate
- Acetate is slightly warmer than viscose.
- It absorbs moisture and is a good conductor of heat
- It can have a lustrous or matt surface.
- It drapes well.
- It neither shrinks nor stretches.
- It recovers quickly from creasing when it is dry.
- It is an easy-care fabric.
- It takes dye well and colour can be introduced at the spinning stage.
- Like viscose, acetate burns very easily so it also has a flame resist finish applied to it.

Tencel
- Tencel is environmentally friendly as it is made from wood pulp from sustainable forests.
- It feels like silk.
- It breathes like cotton.
- It is absorbent.
- It is washable.
- It does not crease as much as linen.

PROPERTIES OF SYNTHETIC FIBRE FABRICS

Polyester
- Polyester is strong, tough and wears well. It resists abrasion.
- It is as strong when wet as it is when dry.
- It is an easy care fabric as it is not harmed by acids, alkalis or bleaches. It needs little or no ironing.
- It does not absorb water.
- It is flame resistant
- It is crease resistant.
- It is thermoplastic and can be permanently pleated.
- It can be made water-repellent. This means it can have a chemical finish applied to it that helps it to repel water; it is not waterproof. A small amount of water will 'run off' the fabric. It is used in shower-proof jackets and coats.

Acrylic

- Acrylic is strong.
- The crimping of the fibres causes the yarn to trap pockets of air making the fabric warmer.
- The fabric can be fine, light in weight or heavier for warmer wear.
- It can be soft and drapes well.
- It can have a dull surface or lustre.
- It can be permanently pleated.

Polyamide (nylon)

- Polyamide is very fine and extremely strong.
- It does not absorb moisture. Moisture runs off it.
- It is crease resistant.
- It is a thermoplastic fabric.
- It is hard wearing and resists abrasion.
- It is an easy care fabric; it washes easily and needs little ironing.
- It is flameproof and will not catch fire, but will melt when it comes into contact with heat.
- The surface of polyamide fabric can be changed by brushing. Brushed polyamide is used for nightwear because it is warm.

Elastane (Lycra)

- Elastane does not absorb moisture.
- It is extremely elastic; it stretches and regains its shape.
- It is lightweight.
- It is used to make aerobic clothing as well as swim wear.

Kevlar (aramid)

- Kevlar is very strong and durable.
- It withstands high temperatures and is flame resistant.
- It is resistant to chemicals.

Examination questions

Q1 *Give **one** reason why fabric made from cotton fibres is often used to make jeans.*

....

Acceptable answer

Any one from:
- because cotton fibre is strong
- because cotton fibre resists abrasion.

Q2 *Explain why cotton fibre fabrics are often used for summer clothing.*

2 marks

....

....

Acceptable answer

Because the fibre absorbs moisture and it then **evaporates quickly making it cool to wear**.

Q3 *State how cotton fibre fabrics are made warmer to wear.*

1 mark

....

Acceptable answer

Any one from:
- they can be brushed
- they can be treated so they become fluffy.

Q4 *Explain **one** reason why linen is used for household products such as tea towels.*

2 marks

....

....

Acceptable answer

Linen is **very absorbent** and is therefore suitable for use where it is needed **to remove water from an item**.

Fabric performance

Q5 Explain **one** reason why linen is a suitable fabric to wear in a hot climate.

2 marks

....

....

Acceptable answer
Because linen **absorbs moisture**, which evaporates **quickly making it cool to wear**.

Q6 Give **two** reasons why linen products need to be handled carefully.

2 marks

....

....

Acceptable answer
- They crease easily.
- There is no elasticity in the fibres, so they split easily.

Q7 Explain **two** reasons why garments made out of wool are suitable for winter clothing.

4 marks

....

....

Acceptable answer
Any two from:
- The **waves in the wool** fibres help to **create pockets, which trap the air** making the garments **warm to wear**.
- Wool will **absorb up to 30 per cent of its weight in moisture** helping to give the fabric **extra warmth**.
- Wool has a **high level of elasticity** and causes garments to **fit the body snugly**, e.g. gloves and hats. This helps to **retain heat**.

(E)xaminer's Tip

When asked to explain two reasons it is important to give two different reasons, not just the same reason explained twice in a different way.

Q8

i) Name **four** pieces of equipment needed to carry out an abrasion test on cotton fabric in a classroom.

....

....

ii) Use notes and sketches to show how this abrasion test will be carried out.

Acceptable answer

i) Any four from:
- jam jar/block
- fabric
- something to secure fabric, e.g. elastic band; string
- abrasive item/pumice stone
- watch/timer/clock.

ii) Any four stages from:
- Cut a piece of fabric large enough to go over a jam jar.
- Retain a control sample.
- Secure fabric with an elastic band.
- Use an abrasive item to rub over the fabric.
- Examine the fabric after a period of time or each set of strokes, e.g. every 5 or 10.
- Record results.
- Evaluate, compared to control sample.

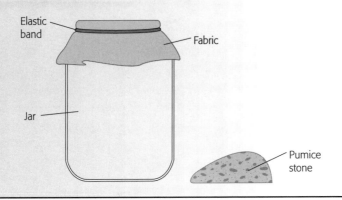

Elastic band

Fabric

Jar

Pumice stone

Q9 *A tent is made from microfibres designed to protect the user from winter weather.*

*Explain **three** advantages of using microfibres for a tent.*

....

....

....

....

....

....

Acceptable answer

Any three from:

- **Thin/fine** therefore **lightweight/reduced volume**.
- **Woven very closely** together therefore increases **windproofing/waterproofing**.
- A good **insulator**, which keeps the air **trapped** inside
- **High moisture transfer** properties therefore allows the fabric to **breathe and reduces condensation**.
- The **blended/mixed polymers retain** and extend the properties of the fibres with which they are blended, therefore **improving performance**.

Examiner's Tip

When answering a technically difficult question you must demonstrate that you have both a knowledge and understanding of the particular part of the specfication. It is not necessary for you to use the exact words within the mark scheme to earn the marks.

You need to know that:

☐ Colour can change fabric appearance.

☐ Decoration can change fabric appearance.

APPLICATION OF COLOUR

Resist dyeing

Where a white pattern is required on a coloured background, the patterned part is printed with a special chemical that will not 'take the dye' – it will resist it – hence the name. Examples of resist dyeing include the following:

Batik: The pattern is applied using wax and the colour is applied using a cold water dye. When the dye is dry the wax is removed by picking off the larger lumps of wax and removing the residue with heat.

Tie-dye: A light coloured fabric is tied in a random pattern and then submerged in a dye bath. When dried the ties are removed and the fabric in these areas remains the original colour.

Silk painting: Silk is stretched on a frame and a gutta pattern is applied to create a barrier, which will resist the silk paint. The paint is applied with a soft brush filling the shape.

Screen printing

A frame is prepared with a fine gauze fabric, which will allow the dye to pass through. The pattern is created by either producing a stencil, which is laid on the fabric, or by imposing a photographic image on the screen. Thick dye is forced through the screen using a squeegee.

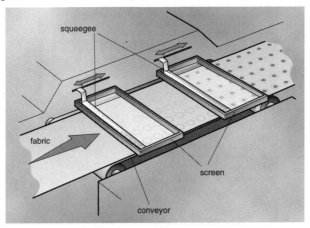

Flat bed screen printing

Block printing

The design is traced onto wood blocks, one for each colour, and the background is cut away. Only that part which is left in relief will be printed. This process is carried out by hand.

Transfer printing

The colour is applied to paper and transferred using heat and pressure.

Digital printing

This involves printing a design developed using CAD. It is achieved by the design being printed on to paper and then transferred on to fabric using heat. The design can also be transferred directly to the fabric.

Fabric printing using a traditional rotary printer

DECORATION OF FABRICS

Decorative stitching

Decorative stitching can be applied by hand or machine. There are many different stitches. Computerised sewing machines allow decorative stitching to be added quickly to items. CAD packages assist in this process.

Appliqué

Appliqué means to apply one fabric to another. The appliqué pattern is cut out, usually stiffened using Vilene® and applied to a background fabric. The edge of the appliqué pattern is held down using a machine satin stitch.

Appliqué work

Quilting

Quilting gives thickness to fabric. It is constructed using three layers; the top layer is the original fabric; the middle layer is polyester wadding and the bottom layer is a backing layer. The three layers are stitched together using either a 'checked' pattern or a random pattern.

Patchwork

Patchwork is the joining of small pieces of fabric to make a larger decorative piece of fabric. The patchwork pieces must be a regular shape, e.g. square, rectangle, triangle etc. The pieces are hemmed together using hand stitching.

Examination questions

Q1 *State in the correct order **four** main stages of producing an appliqué design. The first stage is done for you.*

5 marks

1 Cut out the fabric shapes.

2 ....

3 ....

4 ....

5 ....

Acceptable answer

Any four from:
- stiffen with Vilene®/bondaweb/backing fabric
- attach to fabric/pin/tack
- stitch into place using a satin stitch or hand embroidery
- remove pins or tacking
- press.

Correct order **(1 mark)**

Q2 Describe **three** main stages of the batik process and give a reason why each stage is necessary.

....

....

....

....

....

....

Acceptable answer

Any three from:
- Stage 1: Fabric should be **stretched** on a **frame**.
Reason: to **stabilise** the fabric/hold fabric in place.

- Stage 2: **Liquid/hot wax** applied to create a pattern using **a batik tool/tjanting tool**.
Reason: to stop/resist colours from running into each other.

- Stage 3: **Colour applied** to the fabric **allowing paint/dye to seep** into the fabric.
Reason: to create the design detail.

- Stage 4: When **paint/dye dries** the wax should be **removed**.
Reason: wax is no longer needed.

Fabric appearance

TOPICS

You need to know about:

- ☐ Lay planning and cutting.

- ☐ Joining techniques.

- ☐ Finishing techniques.

- ☐ Construction techniques.

- ☐ Use of critical dimensions and tolerances.

KEY POINTS

LAY PLANNING AND CUTTING

INDUSTRIAL APPLICATION

The fabric is prepared either by folding or leaving as a single layer. The pattern pieces are fitted on to the fabric to ensure little wastage. This is called lay planning. Pattern pieces can be placed on the fold or laid parallel to the selvedge on the straight grain. CAD can be used in industry to plan large-scale production.

Fabric can also have a 'one way' pattern or a pile, which is referred to as a nap. This must be taken into account when cutting fabric to ensure the pattern matches up or the pile on velvet is running in the same direction.

Cutting out needs to be accurate to ensure the fabric is the exact size and shape of the pattern pieces. This helps with quality control. In high volume production, cutting out is done using computerised cutting equipment.

JOINING TECHNIQUES

Joining techniques are used in the construction of textile products. Different methods are used according to where the join will be on the product and the type of fabric.

The plain seam is the simplest of seams. It is constructed by placing the right side of two pieces of fabric together. It is then stitched 1.5 cm from the edge in one-off production and 1 cm from the edge in high volume production. When constructing a plain seam using a woven fabric it is stitched using a straight stitch on the sewing machine with a suitable tension. When sewing a plain seam on knitted fabric it is stitched using a stretch stitch and the machine needle is replaced with a ball point needle. This has a tiny ball on the end of the needle which pushes through the knitting rather than punching through the fibres (as with a normal needle) which can damage the yarn and cause the knitting to ladder.

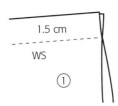

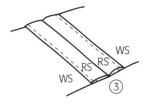

Plain seam

Press open

Bonded seams are used when it is necessary to join together two pieces of fabric but it is not desirable to stitch them. This may be for a variety of reasons including the need for the textiles item to remain completely waterproof or for the seam to be extremely reliable. Fabrics, which have a laminated finish, are often bonded together.

There are two methods for producing this seam – one involves interlinking the seam, the other overlaying the seam. If the seam is being used on a garment where there may be additional strain, the interlinking method will be used.

Bonding involves the use of adhesives, which must be very carefully used during manufacture. The adhesive can bond on contact, which means the construction process must be very accurate, or it can be set by heat.

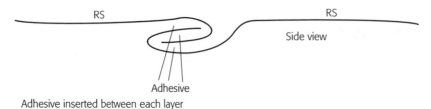

Adhesive inserted between each layer

Interlocking method

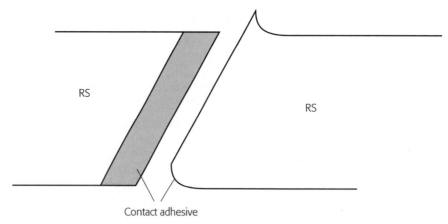

Seam rolled during production to ensure adhesive
is in contact across length of join.

Overlaying method

FINISHING TECHNIQUES

After the seam is constructed the edges of the seam are neatened to improve the quality of the product and to stop the fabric from fraying. The following methods can be used.

- **Zigzag:** The single edges of the fabric are individually stitched using the sewing machine. The stitched used is a zigzag stitch. The size and the width of the stitch are determined by the fabric.

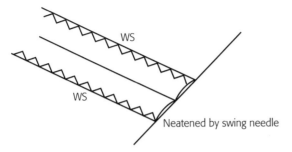

Zigzag stitch

- **Overlocking:** Overlocked seams are constructed using a commercial overlocker. The machine stitches and neatens the seam, and trims any access fabric away as the seam is stitched. The overlocker is also used to stitch knitted fabrics as it can stitch with a stretch stitch. All high volume production lines use an overlocker.

- **Fusing:** Seams can be fused together using adhesive and heat. The seam used is usually an interlocked seam with the glue applied to the joining surfaces. This method is used where a waterproof and/or very strong construction is required.

- **Pressing:** Good quality items are pressed using an iron or a steam press at specific times during production. Seams are pressed after each major construction point to ensure a flat finish.

CONSTRUCTION TECHNIQUES

Construction techniques are used during making to improve the performance of the item.

- **Reinforcing** is used where there is likely be strain on an item, e.g. the top of a pocket; the opening of a duvet cover; the entrance to a tent. Reinforcing can be achieved by adding an additional fabric to improve the structure. These areas are then usually stitched with a double row of stitching or a triangle of stitching to spread the load on the 'strain' area.

Reinforcing of pockets

- **Darts** can be single or double pointed. They are used to remove fullness from an area and to provide shape. The fabric is folded and stitched from the widest point to the narrowest point. Three stitches are made on the fold to avoid any puckers or lumps.

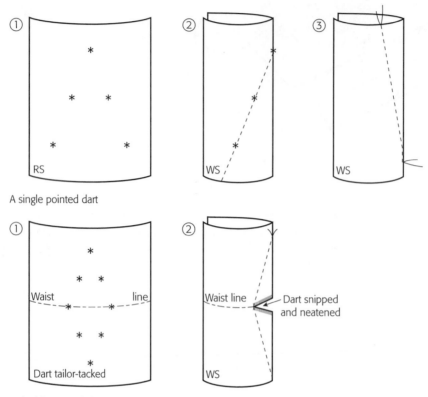

A single pointed dart

A double pointed dart

- **Interfacing** is used to provide 'body' to fabrics. It is used in collars, cuffs and the front openings of shirts and blouses. The interfacing is either ironed or sewn into place. The interfacing is cut without a seam allowance, as this would add bulk to the seam. Iron on interfacing must be pressed carefully into place to avoid stretching. Wherever possible interfacing is attached to a piece of fabric which will not be seen, e.g. the underneath of the collar or cuffs.

- **Lining** is added to the inside of garments, especially coats, jackets, skirts and expensive dresses. It is usually constructed in a fine polyester fabric which has a sheen. It can be a similar colour to the item or striking contrasts can be used as a design feature. The lining is made in the same way as the main garment and attached to the inside, hiding all the construction techniques. This enhances the quality of the product.

USE OF CRITICAL DIMENSIONS AND TOLERANCES

The critical dimensions refer to the size something will be, e.g. the size of a pocket; the finished length of a pair of trousers or the size of a cushion. When cutting fabric for an item, a seam allowance must be added to ensure the critical dimension is achieved. The tolerance refers to the minimum and maximum level of defect that will be accepted, e.g. the minimum/maximum acceptable size of a pocket or the minimum/maximum acceptable size of a seam.

Sidebar: How fabrics are cut, shaped and formed to specific tolerances

Testing seam tolerance

Examination questions

Q1 *Use notes and sketches to show **three** stages of constructing and stitching a plain seam.*

3 marks

Acceptable answer

Diagrams and notes showing the right and wrong side of the fabric and any three from:
- put right sides together
- pin together
- tack and sew 1.5 cm from the edge
- remove tacking
- press seam open.

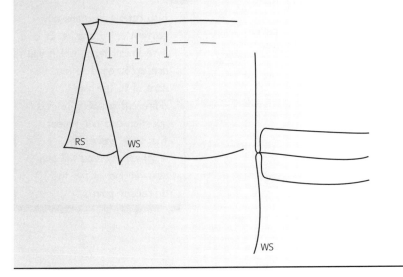

Q2 *Give **two** reasons why it may be necessary to neaten the edge of a seam allowance.*

2 marks

....

....

Acceptable answer

- To provide a good quality/neater finish.
- To prevent the fabric from fraying.

Q3 *Explain **two** points that must be considered when cutting pattern pieces from checked fabric.*

4 marks

....

....

....

....

Acceptable answer

Any two from:
- Ensure straight grain is maintained to keep checks straight.
- Ensure the notches are on the same check pattern.
- Take account of the nap to ensure checks match.

 xaminer's Tip

Nap refers to a one-way pattern or to checks. It is a technical term, which you are encouraged to use. Be careful to use two different answers to this question and not repeat the same answer in another way. You will only gain full marks for two different points.

TOPICS

You need to know about:

□ commercial patterns.

□ patterns.

□ standard components.

COMMERCIAL PATTERNS

Commercial patterns are sold in envelopes, which have a picture of the item on the front and the fabric and component requirements on the back. The pattern is produced in thin paper with each of the pattern pieces printed on the paper. Each pattern envelope includes an instruction sheet.

Commercial patterns use the following symbols to provide instructions.

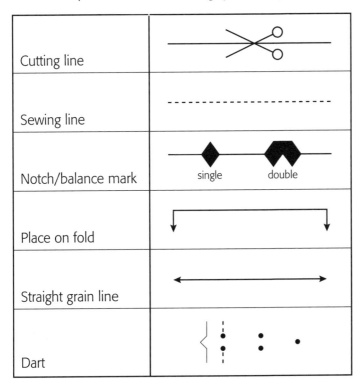

Cutting line	
Sewing line	
Notch/balance mark	single double
Place on fold	
Straight grain line	
Dart	

PATTERNS

INDUSTRIAL APPLICATION

• **Drafting flat patterns:** After designing a textile product the pattern pieces need to be created. This is called pattern drafting. The design is mathematically transferred on to paper. Patterns are produced to standard sizes and may need adjusting to fit individuals. Every pattern is created to match critical dimensions which are used throughout the textiles industry. The technical name for these patterns are 'block patterns'.

- **Adapting commercial patterns:** Adjustments to commercial patterns can be made before the fabric is cut out to improve the fit of the garment. The adjustments can include changing the length of a garment, e.g. the legs of trousers, the length of a skirt or the length of sleeves. Some adjustments can only be made when trying on the garment, e.g. increasing or decreasing the size of darts. The paper pattern is pinned onto the fabric following the instructions and cut out. The fabric pieces must be exactly the same shape as the paper pattern or the pieces will not fit together. Each pattern piece is 'matched' together using the notches or balance marks.

- **Prototypes:** Before batch and high volume production takes place, designs are tested by producing a prototype of the textile item. This is evaluated to ensure it matches the designer's expectations. The prototype can be modelled using 3D paper models to test the flat pattern. The garment is also tested in a cheap fabric, usually calico. This is called a toile.

STANDARD COMPONENTS

Standard components are used to complete a garment, e.g. fastenings. They are produced commercially and bought in by manufacturers. Standard components include zips, Velcro, buttons and press fasteners.

- **Zips** can be used to fasten jackets, trousers and skirts, blouses and dresses as well as openings in cushions or bags.

- **Velcro** 'sticks' two sections of fabric together using a hooking system, which sticks to a fluffy area. Velcro is often used on children's clothing as well as shoes and bags. Sports skirts are often fastened using Velcro.

- **Buttons** are produced in many colours and shapes and can be made into a decorative feature. In order to fasten, a button needs a buttonhole. Buttons are often attached to the front of blouses, shirts, coats, jackets and are also used on dungarees and the back of dresses, bags, cushion covers and duvet covers.

- **Press fasteners** are made from either metal or plastic. They are in two parts with one half having a circular section that snaps into a similar shape in the other. Each part must be attached accurately to ensure correct closure of the garment. Used on items that need to be fastened and opened quickly and have an exactly positioned, secure but non-bulky fastening like baby wear, detachable rain hoods and duvet covers.

Examination questions

Q1 *Name **two** different standard components that could be used to fasten a jacket.*

2 marks

....

....

Acceptable answer
Any two from:
- zip
- velcro
- buttons

Q2 Use notes and sketches to show **four** main stages of inserting a zip into the centre back seam of a dress.

Acceptable answer

Sketches and notes that show any four from:
- Turn under seam allowance.
- Tack or press the seam into place.
- Pin and/or tack the zip into place (so the zip cannot be seen and the seam meets in the middle of the zip).
- Change the presser foot on the machine to a zipper foot.
- Stitch the zip into place ensuring the stitching is not too close to the zip.
- Remove tacking.

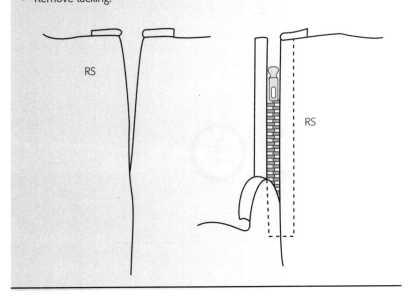

Q3 Use notes and sketches to show **three** stages of attaching a button to the front of a cotton poplin shirt.

3 marks

....

....

....

Acceptable answer

- Place the button to ensure it matches the buttonhole.
- Stitch through the button forming a single or double bar on the reverse of the fabric.
- Buttonhole stitch through the bar to secure the button.

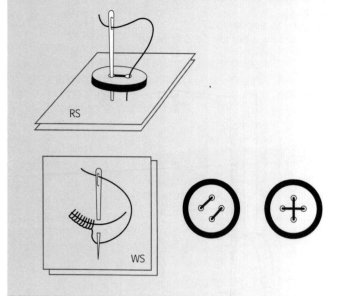

TOPICS

You need to know about:

☐ Risk assessment.

☐ The safe use of tools and equipment.

KEY POINTS

By law all products must be produced in a safe environment. This law that enforces this is the Health and Safety at Work Act (1974). All manufacturers have a Health and Safety officer to ensure that the workplace is set up in a safe way.

RISK ASSESSMENT

The Health and Safety officer must examine the workplace and judge whether there are any hazards which may make the workplace unsafe. This is called risk assessment.

The Health and Safety officer will check all electrical equipment to make sure it is safe and correctly positioned. They will also check safety guards on machinery, making sure workers are wearing ear muffs in a noisy workplace, and that masks are worn where fumes are created, e.g. in a print room where dyes are being used. Other safety checks could include ensuring long hair is tied back to avoid it getting caught in machinery, and ensuring the use of machinery does not disturb other workers. The Health and Safety officer will also check that chairs for specific equipment are the correct height, and that ventilation, heating and lighting are adequate.

SAFE USE OF TOOLS AND EQUIPMENT

• **Tools** can have sharp edges, e.g. scissors, and so need to be handled with care. Cutting during manufacture can be carried out using CAM thus reducing the possibilities of accidents.

• **Equipment** includes such items as sewing machines and irons. These should carry the BEAB mark of safety and must be checked annually. The correct plug and fuse must be used. Cables must not be trailing along the ground as they may be tripped over. Sockets must not be overloaded and electrical equipment must be kept away from water.

Safety rules also apply when working at school or at home.

Hazard and warning symbols you may see at school

Examination questions

Q1 *Give **three** safety rules that should be applied when using a sewing machine.*

3 marks

....

....

....

Acceptable answer

Any three from:
- Tie hair back when using a machine.
- Do not distract the machine operator.
- Work in good light.
- Ensure cables are secured to the floor.
- Ensure cables cannot be tripped over.

Q2 *Explain the purpose of risk assessment in industry.*

2 marks

....

....

Acceptable answer

To judge whether there is a **hazard** that will make the workplace **unsafe**.

You need to know:

☐ How ICT is used in single item production.

☐ How computer aided design (CAD) is used in textile technology for single item products.

KEY POINTS

Using a computer speeds up the time it takes to carry out a task. ICT can be used:

- developing detailed specifications

- developing design ideas

- modifying design ideas

- communicating ideas to manufacturers

- producing detailed work schedules.

USE OF ICT IN SINGLE ITEM PRODUCTION

Developing specifications: When researching, the Internet is a useful tool for gathering a range of information together. Many manufacturers have web pages which supply information on product ranges and fabrics. Manufacturers can supply information on request, and will answer specific questions on prices and availability of products via e-mail.

Spreadsheets: When developing specifications, consumer views can be recorded using spreadsheets. This allows analysis to take place and results to be reported using graphical methods (graphs and charts). Spreadsheets can also be used for costing and cost analysis.

Clipart libraries contain hundreds of images and illustrations which can be used as starting points for design ideas or can be adapted to meet a specific design need. This facility can be used for fashion garments or decoration of textile products.

CD ROMs contain a mass of digital information which can be interactive allowing the user to progress through problems or ideas. There are many comprehensive databases stored on CD ROMs. Databases operate in columns or fields and allow the user to sort the information in many different ways. They can also be used for costing and cost analysis.

Scanners are used to import images into text or change the image by enhancing it through a computer package. Scanners are a useful tool when producing design ideas. They can be used in digital printing to produce a design idea onto transfer paper.

Digital cameras store images on a removeable storage disk. The images can be enhanced or manipulated using a computer. These images can be pasted into documents or printed from the storage disk on to high sheen paper.

Developing and modifying design ideas: Computer aided design (CAD) is used to develop and edit design ideas. Designs can be drawn, adapted and coloured using these packages. This allows the designer to work quickly and make rapid changes. Designs can also be viewed using a range of colours in order to achieve the desired effect. The packages also allow tone and shading to be used and it is possible to scan in fabric samples to get a clear idea of how the textile product will look when it is manufactured.

Designing fabric using CAD

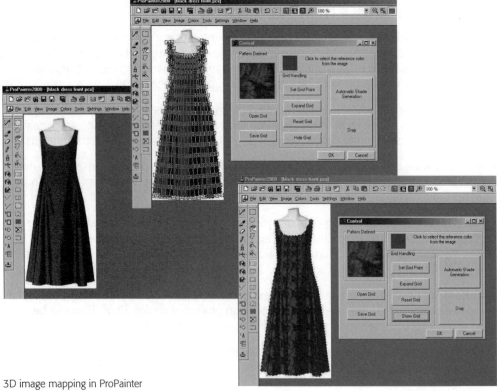

3D image mapping in ProPainter

Use of ICT and CAD in single item production

Communicating ideas to clients and manufacturers: This can be done in a range of ways. Information can be e-mailed for a quick efficient transfer of ideas. CAD packages can also be used to present design ideas to clients, demonstrating a high level of presentation skills. Technically the packages can also show specific construction details to help the manufacturer of the product.

Producing detailed work schedules: This can be achieved through e-mail and computerised Gantt charts to ensure production is planned in order to save time and money. Spreadsheets can also be used for costing and cost analysis.

USING CAD IN SINGLE ITEM PRODUCTION

CAD is used in textile technology for single item products. It is used in the initial stages of production to develop exclusive design ideas for the client to view. This method allows the designer to make instant changes to the idea with the client watching the results. Each idea can be saved so that earlier ideas can be returned to and reviewed.

CAD can also be used to demonstrate methods of enhancing or decorating the design idea by including embroidery or beadwork. With the aid of a CAD program the enhancement can be moved or adapted according to the client's wishes. From the design ideas the pattern pieces can be drafted and plotted using the CAD package, although on single exclusive items this is still often done by a qualified pattern drafter/cutter.

Examination questions

Q1 *Give **three** advantages of using a CAD package when designing an exclusive, one-off evening dress.*

3 marks

....

....

....

Acceptable answer

Any three from:

- Design changes can be made easily.
- The product can be viewed in different colour ways.
- The dimensions can be increased or decreased.

Q2 Explain **one** way in which CAD would be used to ensure efficient working practice in the cutting out of pattern pieces.

....

....

Acceptable answer

The program would allow the **pattern layout to be plotted** to ensure **minimum fabric wastage**, thus **reducing costs** to the manufacturer.

xaminer's Tip

Single items are usually exclusive products that are made by a designer for a specific client. Single item production can also refer to the items you made in the classroom where you have chosen the design (or commercial pattern) and the type and colour of fabric making it exclusive to you and a 'one-off product' or 'single item production'.

Q3 Spreadsheets are an efficient modelling tool used when designing.

Describe **two** specific ways in which a spreadsheet can be used in the single item production of a textiles product.

4 marks

1 ....

....

2 ....

....

Acceptable answer

Any two from:
- **recording and storing for future use data/analysing data** collected **from questionnaires and surveys of existing products**;
- **preparing a cost analysis** of **different ideas/a developed idea**.

xaminer's Tip

The question gives you a generic way of using spreadsheets. To access the marks you must make sure that your answers are *specific* uses, examples of which are given in the sample answers above.

Q4 *A printer is one piece of equipment used with a computer. It produces 'hard copy' of screen images and can help when developing design ideas.*

2 marks

*Name **two** other items of equipment that can be used with a computer to help in the development of design ideas.*

1 ....

2 ....

Acceptable answer

Any two from:
- Scanner
- Digital camera
- Video camera

 xaminer's Tip

The question asks for items of equipment, these are generally described as 'hardware'. Items of software such as clipart libraries, CAD packages and CD-ROMS would **not** score marks.

Q5 *A scanner can be used when developing design ideas.*

2 marks

*Describe **one** way in which a scanner is used when developing design ideas for a textiles product.*

....

....

Acceptable answer

To **scan in a prepared design/series of designs** to enable **a graphics package to be used to add details of colour/tone/style features/ scans of fabric for further evaluation**.

 xaminer's Tip

The question asks how a scanner is used in the development of a textiles product. Your answer must state the stage of the designing process, for example **scan in a prepared design**, and how you would use the scanned image, for example **to use a graphics package to develop the design further**.

You need to know that:

☐ Computer aided manufacture (CAM) is the use of computer-controlled machinery to manufacture a product.

☐ CAM is useful in the production of quality products for domestic use.

COMPUTER AIDED MANUFACTURE (CAM)

Computer aided manufacture (CAM) is where a computer program is written to control the machine operation to be carried out. Often design data is transferred digitally, direct from a CAD package, but where this is not the case precise data must be prepared for the computer program. It must always be remembered that the output from any computer controlled machine is only as accurate as the program data.

THE USE OF CAM IN A DOMESTIC SETTING

In domestic production it is also possible to employ CAM techniques. Computerised sewing machines and transfer printing can be used in small scale or single item production.

CAM helps to:

• save time
• ensure consistent results
• ensure the production of a good quality product.

Transfer printing is achieved using both CAD and CAM. A design is transferred onto specially coated paper and the image is then pressed using heat on to the required place on a textile item. Hundreds of items can be produced in a short space of time.

Flat pattern drafting allows patterns to be produced using basic blocks which match critical dimensions. Flat patterns can be produced for hats, bags, fashion accessories, soft furnishings and garments. This saves time and fabric, as the computer will carry out the mathematical calculations to ensure success. Pattern pieces can be plotted on to an appropriate material before being used to cut out the fabric.

Computerised sewing machines have many functions, including decorative stitches. Designs can be programmed into the sewing machine and stored in the sewing machine's

Super Galaxie sewing machine

memory. Once set up the machine will embroider the design idea. Using a domestic machine allows one colour to be embroidered at a time. The memory will distinguish the different colour needs. When the machine has completed one colour you must change the thread and begin with a new colour. Using industrial machines means that several colours can be threaded up together and the design is produced simultaneously.

Using CAM means that items will be consistent, as the cutting out of pattern pieces and the stitching of a design idea will be the same each time. The control over the product is programmed in thus ensuring hundreds of identical items. This is essential when producing items such as badges for school uniforms or a manufacturing logo. CAM removes the 'human error' factor.

A laser fabric cutter in a textiles factory

Examination questions

Q1   *Give **three** advantages of using CAM to aid single item production.*   3 marks

1 ....

2 ....

3 ....

Acceptable answer
Saves time.
Ensures consistent results.
Enables the production of a good quality product.

Q2 Give **three** advantages of using a flat pattern drafting program during single item production.

1 ....

2 ....

3 ....

Acceptable answer

Saves time.
Computer carries out mathematical calculations.
Fabrics can be economically used as the program plots out the pattern pieces.

Examiner's Tip

Make sure your answers are relevant for single item production and do not refer to high volume production.

Q3 Computer aided manufacture can be used in the process of 'transfer printing' a one-off image onto fabric.

Explain **one** advantage of using CAM, rather than manual methods, when transfer printing a one-off image onto fabric.

....

....

Acceptable answer

The **image to be printed on the fabric must be reversed for printing onto the transfer paper**, this is much **easier and faster to perform accurately using a computer system** than by manual methods.

You need to know that:

☐ The target market group and the product specification determine the scale of production.

☐ The name given to individual items is called one-off production.

☐ For most textile items batch production will be used.

☐ Within batch production different production systems are used.

☐ For a large number of items to be produced a high volume production system will be used.

KEY POINTS

Textiles items can be produced as unique one-off items through to thousands of items for the High Street retailers. The numbers that are produced depend on a range of factors determined by the target market and include the following:

- how exclusive the product is
- the cost of production
- the profit margin.

ONE-OFF PRODUCTION

This is very customer focused and often a client will speak directly to the designer and the specific requirements will be taken into account at all stages of production. The client is consulted when the design is completed; when the fabrics are selected and during the making process. The client will have a fitting for the item to ensure the 'perfect fit'. This is an expensive process which most people cannot afford. Film stars and the Royal family are examples of people who will have one-off products made exclusively for them. Other items include catwalk dresses, designer outfits and bespoke tailored suits. Occasionally people will have a very special item made for them, such as their wedding dress.

One-off production is expensive as highly skilled tailors or seamstresses do a lot of the work by hand. Although a sewing machine will be used during production, parts of the garments will be hand stitched, e.g. linings into jackets, beadwork on to dresses and hand-worked buttonholes.

BATCH PRODUCTION

This type of production is used when there needs to be a quantity of items for a specific market. Any item of school uniform with a crest or a badge on it is produced using batch production. All the items will be identical to ensure uniformity. The workforces who are involved in batch production are highly skilled as they must be able to produce the different orders that come into the factory. The workers are organised into 'cells' or teams and every worker must be able to complete all the tasks required within a team (the workers are multi-skilled). Other items that are batch produced include bags, fashion items, coats and 'event targeted' items such as Christmas hats or Jubilee items.

HIGH VOLUME PRODUCTION

This type of production is used to produce items where thousands of identical products are required. Production is continuous and uses highly efficient machinery to ensure products are produced 24 hours a day, seven days a week. Where there is a continuous flow production line the workforce is usually small, as a lot of the process will be automated. The workforce will be trained to do one job only and they will perform that job well. The textile product will be moved around the factory floor for each stage to be completed, e.g. the collar will be attached to a shirt in one location; the sleeves will be attached at another location on the factory floor, the cuff will be attached to the sleeve elsewhere; and the buttonholes will be completed on the shirt somewhere different again. Textiles products that are made using high volume production include socks, tights and standard items of underwear.

PRODUCTION SYSTEMS

A system is made up of parts or activities, which must be connected in an organised way. A production system is a combination of several activities which all rely on each other.

- A **straight-line system** is used in high volume production and the item flows through a number of workstations (organised in a straight line). The worker or operator performs the same operation (task) hundreds of times a day and then passes the item on to the next operator for their input. The work is synchronised so that every operation takes the same amount of time. This is called line balancing. This system often involves the use of CAM.

- In a **sectional system** the workers are divided into teams (or sections) which deal with one part of the production of the product. The team completes the task between them before passing it on to the next section. This system needs a large amount of factory space as the teams are organised in a U shape.

- A **progressive bundle system** uses parts of the straight line and sectional systems. Operators are arranged in teams but the work is balanced. It is a very flexible system as it can cope with frequent style changes, small batches and short delivery times. The products usually remain in bundles until they are assembled enough to hang on rails.

- A **quick response system** allows manufacturers to respond quickly to market change and adapt or change their production techniques. The work is arranged in small bundles and the operators stand up to work and move from one machine to another in a workstation. The machinists or operators need to be highly skilled. They are highly motivated as they work together to achieve high turnover and pay is often productivity related.

- A **unit production system (UPS)** is another quick response system which handles single items and operates on a power-driven loop. The work is fed around the loop on hangers, which are addressed to the next section of production and have the details of the next operation to take place. When the operator finishes their work the item is sent around the loop to the next address. This system is entirely computer controlled allowing each garment to be tracked within the system.

Examination questions

Q1 *High volume production is used in the textiles industry.*
Describe what is meant by 'high volume production'.

2 marks

....

....

Acceptable answer

The production line operates **24 hours a day** to produce **identical products in large quantities**.

Q2 *Name **one** suitable method of production for each of the following textiles items.*

4 marks

(a) *School blazer badge*

....

(b) *Tights*

....

(c) *Fashion evening dress*

....

(d) *Exclusive wedding dress*

....

Acceptable answer

a Batch production
b High volume production
c Batch production
d One-off production

Q3 *Explain **two** ways in which the introduction of technology in the textiles industry has affected employment.*

4 marks

Acceptable answer

Any two from:
- There has been **an increase in the amount of machinery** because of the development of ICT – this has led to a **reduction in the size of the workforce**.
- A reduction in the size of the workforce has led to a **reduction of the wages bill** – this **reduces ongoing costs and can lead to increased profits**.
- The **workforce has had to retrain** to develop the **new skills** necessary to operate new equipment.

xaminer's Tip

When answering a technical question you must demonstrate that you have both a knowledge and understanding of the particular part of the specfication. It is not necessary for you to use the exact words within the mark scheme to earn the marks.

TOPICS

You need to know that:

☐ ICT can contribute to an efficient production system thus reducing waste and costs.

☐ ICT can increase the speed of output including easy and fast communication.

☐ ICT can assist in ensuring consistency and high quality products.

☐ ICT can aid the monitoring of quality textile products.

EFFICIENT PRODUCTION SYSTEMS

Quality: An effective computerised system improves production levels and the quality of production. A computerised system allows all stages of production to be monitored and helps in the reduction of human errors, which, in turn, can save potentially wasted time and materials.

Production systems: Computers can help in the planning of efficient production systems or be part of these systems. The textiles industry uses systems for many different purposes. The choice of system is influenced by many different factors, i.e. the type of product; how many are being made; the delivery time scale; the size of the factory and the size and skills of the work force.

Modelling: The use of 2D modelling can assist in creating a fast and efficient manufacturing process. This facility is used in batch production where it is necessary for the manufacturer to respond quickly to changes in demand. A design can be created on the computer and viewed in different fabrics and colours. The programs allow the product to be turned and viewed from different angles. Changing the fabric of a product will change the hang and the drape and this can be clearly seen from the computer screen. Although the image is 2D the item 'comes to life' and appears to be a 3D 'virtual' product on the screen.

Communication: This use of ICT can reduce costs by avoiding unnecessary time wasting. Once the design has been approved by the client it can be e-mailed to the manufacturer. This high-speed communication technique is essential in the fashion industry, as companies need to be the market leaders in order to maximise the profit margin.

Stock control: Computers are an important link in ensuring both manufacturers and retailers can keep the correct amount of stock in either the factory or the warehouse. Manufacturers need to have the correct amount of fabric, thread and components and they need accurate records of the amount they have in stock. Items cannot be constructed without the constituent parts. A manufacturer cannot put the zip into a skirt if the stock of zips has run out. Similarly manufacturers do not have the space to stock-pile threads, fabric and components, so the ordering of stock at the correct time is critical. ICT can assist this process ensuring stock is automatically ordered when stocks are reduced to a predetermined level.

INCREASED SPEED OF OUTPUT

The speed of output is very important to manufacturers, as time of production is linked to cost and profits. The longer an item is in production the more money it costs the manufacturer. It is important to sell the product as quickly as possible to recoup the moneys already spent during production. Any job within the textiles industry which has to be undertaken by manpower, can increase the labour costs.

Using a range of CAD and CAM techniques can vastly increase the speed of output.

- CAD will allow the reviewing, adapting or changing of designs to be quickly achieved rather than going back to an empty piece of paper and starting again. Each image can be stored and called up when required.
- CAM will allow fast machines to carry out intricate processes consistently rather than being carried out by hand.
- The use of e-mail allows quick dispatch and instant receipt of information rather than sending information in the overland postal system, which can take several days.

CONSISTENT AND HIGH QUALITY PRODUCTS

- **Computer integrated manufacture (CIM):** In this system both CAD and CAM are integrated to allow a fully automated production process with every aspect of manufacture controlled by computer. Powerful CAD systems can be linked to the CIM system allowing the entire design development, production schedule and manufacturing operation to be undertaken in one single system. Manufacturers who adopt this system can make dramatic reductions in the production costs of their products and increase their quality and reliability.

  This use of ICT also ensures that all products are produced to exactly the same specification and each product is identical. This is a very important factor in both batch and high volume production, which rely on selling high quality identical products. This raises consumer confidence; they know the manufacturer is reliable and the quality of the product is high. An example of this is where CAD data is transferred direct to a laser cutter. Here the fabric is automatically cut to the required shape by the laser using the data from the CAD system.

- **Computer numerical control (CNC):** This system allows machine tools to be independently programmed, and data to be transferred to other computers, thus forming a complex automated production system. This is particularly effective where a number of smaller manufacturers specialise in the making of a component which contributes to a whole product. Again the manufacturer can be confident of the quality of production and the quality of the component. This helps to reduce cost, as the quality of the work or component does not have to be rejected at a later stage of production.

- **Flat pattern making and grading:** In batch and volume production the CAD program can be used to draft the pattern pieces in the same way as in single item production. The

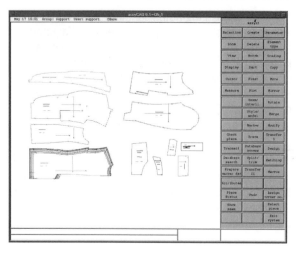

Grading

The use of ICT and CAD/CAM in batch and volume production

program can also be used to grade the pattern, i.e. produce a pattern for each of the standard sizes (e.g. ladies dress sizes 8–20) in the UK. When this job was done by hand it was very time consuming. Grading is carried out without the inclusion of seam allowances as these are added later.

- **Lay planning:** This is very important when batch or high volume production is taking place, as it is essential that wastage is kept to a minimum. Pattern pieces can be fitted together to ensure little fabric is wasted and therefore reduce the costs for the manufacturer. This operation can be completed on the computer before the information is electronically sent to the factory floor. Computerised lay planning allows the company to give a very accurate cost to a job, as the exact quantities of fabric needed can be calculated.

- **Repeatable processes:** These are necessary in both high volume and batch production. A process may need to be repeated hundreds of times and each time it must be both accurate and identical to the one produced before and the one produced afterwards. CAM can assist in this process as the exact requirements can be programmed into the machinery, e.g. the design of a logo or school badge. The machinery ensures a very fast output of products.

MONITORING QUALITY

ICT can also be used to monitor the quality of a product within acceptable critical tolerance levels. This reduces the amount of human input, although to date ICT has not replaced all human quality control checks. Knitting machines have stitch sensors fitted to them in order to regulate the fabric. As knitted fabric is used for many textiles products this is an important development. The aim of quality control is to achieve zero defects by predicting the failure of a machine before it happens. The use of automated testing machines and the electronic gathering of data and its analysis can identity problems very quickly. This in turn leads to higher standards of quality and less wastage.

Examination questions

Q1 *Give **two** ways in which CAD/CAM can aid pattern cutting in batch production.*

2 marks

....

....

Acceptable answer

Any two from:
- A CAD program can be used to draft the pattern pieces.
- CAD can be used to grade the pattern pieces.
- CAM can cut hundreds of layers of fabric at the same time.

Q2 *Explain **one** reason why a designer may use 2D modelling during batch production.*

2 marks

....

....

Acceptable answer

Any one from:
- It will allow the client to see the item in **different colours** and help to **decide the colour ways**.
- The garment or item can be seen from **every angle** thus ensuring the **hang and the shape is correct**.

Q3 *School badges are to be produced to go on to bags.*

*Explain **one** way in which CAD would aid this process.*

2 marks

....

....

Acceptable answer

Any one from:
- CAD would allow the **design** (or elements of the design) **to be adjusted** in size to **improve and enhance the design idea**.
- CAD would allow the designer to make **changes to the colour of the design in a quick and efficient manner**, therefore **saving time**.

Q4 *Explain **two** ways in which CAM could be used during the process of high volume production of an appliqué item.*

4 marks

1 ....

....

2 ....

....

Acceptable answer

Any two of the following:
- CAM allows **bulk cutting** of the fabric pieces and therefore **increases the speed** of production.
- CAM ensures the appliqué pieces are **identical** in **shape and size**.
- CAM allows production of the **satin stitch to be programmed** thus **increasing production speed and accuracy**.
- CAM can **reduce waste** and therefore **save money**.

Section 3
Assessment
Objective 3

You should be aware that:

☐ Consumers have rights and responsibilities.

☐ Manufactuers must maintain a standard.

☐ Product reliability is important.

KEY POINTS

A consumer is anyone who buys commercially produced products, hires an item for a short or long period of time or uses a service. The consumer is the end user and has rights with regard to the function and performance of the item.

CONSUMER RIGHTS AND RESPONSIBILITIES

The law protects the consumer should anything go wrong with the product they buy and use. There are several laws which protect the consumer, and each law has a different function:

• Sale of Goods Act (1979) amended by the Sale and Supply of Goods Act (1994).

• Trades Descriptions Act (1968).

• Trade Marks Act (1994).

The **Sale of Goods Act (1979)** states that a product 'must be of satisfactory quality' and 'fit for its purpose'. The product must reach a reasonable standard in relationship to its cost and any other circumstance. This includes the product's appearance and finish, as well as the safety and the product's durability.

Goods must be fault free, except where they have been sold with the fault clearly marked. Packaging plays an important part in the sale of products and the item inside the packaging must exactly match the description on the packaging. If an item is said to be 100 per cent wool it must be made out of 100 per cent wool.

The Sale of Goods Act applies to all items bought through shops, catalogues, mail order, street markets and door-to-door salespeople.

The **Trades Descriptions Act (1968)** ensures that products are sold 'as described'. What a retailer tells the consumer about a product must be true.

The **Trade Marks Act (1994)** protects the trademarks of companies. It is illegal to use a trademark that does not belong to you. If you buy a product with a company logo stitched on to it, even for a very cheap price, and it turns out to be a fake you are protected by the Trade Marks Act.

MANUFACTURING STANDARDS

Manufacturers must maintain a standard and the British Standards Institute (BSI) tests all kinds of products to ensure they meet the standards laid down. If the BSI has approved them they are awarded the kitemark. The kitemark requires safety information to be displayed on the product and any possible hazard for the consumer to be indicated.

BSI kitemark

Many products also carry the CE mark, which is the European Safety Standard mark. The manufacturer has to carry out tests on the product to ensure there are no safety issues such as sharp edges or loose parts that could come off and choke a child. Young children are particularly at risk from textiles products. All children's items should carry the CE mark, especially toys.

PRODUCT RELIABILITY

All products must be reliable and perform as they are expected to, even after washing or cleaning. Inside or attached to every textiles product is a care label, which gives clear instructions as to how an item must be cared for. The care symbols are used internationally and an agreed code has been adopted, with each symbol having a specific meaning. The International Textile Care Labelling Code (ITCLC) makes it easier to choose the correct method of cleaning for each textile item. Care labels must be permanently fixed to the textiles product. A care label must carry the following information:

- fibre content (this is compulsory)
- any special treatments or finishes
- cleaning instructions
- size of garment.

Washing		Washing continued		Ironing	
Symbol	Meaning	Symbol	Meaning	Symbol	Meaning
40°	Maximum temperature 40° C Mechanical action normal Rinsing and spinning normal	⊠	Do not wash	⌐○	Cool iron
		△Cl	Chlorine bleach can be used	⌐○○	Warm iron
40°	Maximum temperature 40° C Mechanical action reduced Rinse with gradual cooling Spinning reduced	⊠	Do not bleach	⌐○○○	Hot iron
				⊠	Do not iron

Drying		Dry cleaning	
Symbol	Meaning	Symbol	Meaning
40° (Maximum temperature 40° C Mechanical action much reduced Rinsing/Spinning normal)	○	Tumble drying beneficial	Ⓐ	Dry clean in all solvents
	⊠	Do not tumble dry	Ⓟ	Dry clean in perchloroethylene
	|||	Drip dry, soaking wet	Ⓕ	Dry clean in certain solvents only
Hand wash only	—	Dry flat		
	⊡	Hang to dry	⊠	Do not dry clean

Textile care labelling code

Examination questions

 All clothing contains a care label.

i) *The diagram below shows a care label for a pair of denim jeans.*

98% COTTON
2% ELASTANE

*List the **four** pieces of information given by this label.*

1 ....

2 ....

3 ....

4 ....

Acceptable answer

i) Any four from:
1 Temperature at which to wash the jeans.
2 Temperature to use iron.
3 Do not tumble dry.
4 Do not bleach.
5 Do not dry clean.
6 Fibre content of product.

 xaminer's Tip

Textiles labels provide lots of information. You must look carefully at the label and interpret the data. All textiles labels refer to washing/cleaning instructions and care information to ensure the product performs to the expected standard. It provides vital information to the user about this product.

Q2 *The European Safety Standards allow manufacturers to include their CE mark on approved textile products.*

*Explain **one** advantage to the consumer of a manufacturer displaying the CE mark on a soft toy designed for young children.*

....

....

Acceptable answer

The consumer knows that the toy **does not have the potential to harm** young children because it has been **tested to the prescribed European safety standards**.

You should be aware that:

☐ Smart fabrics are being developed.

☐ Finishes can change classic fabrics.

☐ Fabric can change colour.

SMART FABRICS

Originally fabrics were made from natural fibres and the user had to live with the properties they provided. Now fabrics are developed for functional applications, in other words the end use of the fabric determines the functional properties that will be developed. These are called **smart fabrics**.

Smart materials can sense and react to the environment. They can be classified into groups of textile products such as; industrial fabrics, medical textiles, composite reinforcements, filtration fabrics and protective clothing. The whole group is called **technical textiles**. Through the correct choice of fibres, yarns, manufacturing techniques and finishes the desired fabric is engineered.

Bio polishing

This is a process which has been developed using the enzyme cellulase. It is used to improve production methods and for fabric finishes. One of the oldest applications in the textiles industry is that of the enzyme amylases which is used to remove starch size. The warp threads of fabrics are often coated in starch in order to prevent them breaking during weaving. This can cause pilling. Cellulase is used to prevent pilling and improve the smoothness, softness and colour brightness of cotton fabrics.

For cotton fabrics the use of bio polishing is optional for upgrading the fabric. This is not the case for the fabric Tencel. Because it is made from wood pulp, there is a tendency for it to fibrillate easily when wet – this means the surface of the fibres peel up. If the fibrils are not removed the garment will end up covered in pills. This is why Tencel fabric is treated with the enzyme cellulase to enhance its attractive silky appearance.

Technical textiles are not always visible and are often only part of a product or construction. They can be used in the following ways:

• Insulating homes by wrapping the walls of buildings to prevent damage from damp.

• Strengthening car tyres.

• Geotextiles make a firm motorway foundation.

• Finely knitted textile tubes can replace arteries and veins.

• Non-woven fabrics are used in vacuum cleaners as filters.

Other widely used smart textiles include the following:

- Wrinkle-free fabrics, which are used to make garments.

- Clothing for radiation purposes.

- Sanitised fabrics for sportswear and socks, which contain microbial and anti-bacterial protection from sweat.

- Intelligent polymer systems, e.g. the smart bra that changes its properties in response to movement, giving better support when needed. The fabric contains sensors, which measure movement and store information in a microchip. It is this that signals to the polymer fabric to expand or contract.

- Kevlar is a smart material which is five times stronger than steel but much lighter. It is used for bullet-proof vests, flak jackets and other protective clothes.

NEW FINISHES

Technology has helped to developed fabric finishes. Instead of washing jeans with stones to take the 'new look' out of them they are now washed in an enzyme called cellulase. This enzyme is derived from a tropical fungus which breaks down the cellulose in the denim and helps to fade the dye. The result is faded jeans.

COLOUR CHANGES

Fabrics now have the ability to change colour. This technique can be used for a range of reasons; it may be to warn against an exposure to ultra violet rays or to adapt to a change in surroundings. Combat uniforms are only effective if they blend in with their environment; camouflage clothing will not blend in with the snow and ice of the Arctic. Finishes have now been developed which can change colour to blend into their surroundings.

Heat responsive change

The uses of these smart fabrics are increasing as technology develops. Heat-generating fibres respond to the environment by changing colour to fit the surroundings. This happens by using thermochromic leucodyes – pigments which are micro-encapsulated for stability. At room temperature the leucodye, its waxy shell and an acid developer hold together and the pigment keeps its colour. But, when warmed, the wax-like shell melts and the dye and developer separate. As a result, the leucodye becomes colourless. When the temperature cools the wax hardens and the micro-encapsulate becomes whole again. These fabrics may be used for oven gloves to indicate heat, or even fashion-wear.

Light responsive change

Smart fabrics can also change in response to light, one use of which would be clothing that warns of over exposure to sunlight. These UV sensitive fabrics are made using UV sensitive photochromic inks. Photochromic inks are not pigments, they ar dyes which absorb light. Normal inks, on the other hand, contain light reflective pigments. Ultra violet light alters the molecular structure of photochromic inks, causing them to absorb colour. When the UV light is removed, the inks return to their original structure and colour.

Examination questions

 Q1 *Cellulase is an enzyme used in textile production.*
Describe how it is used to change the colour of denim fabric.

2 marks

....

....

Acceptable answer

Cellulase is used to **break down the cellulose** in denim giving the fabric **a faded look** and therefore the fabric becomes light in colour.

xaminer's Tip

Be careful not to mix up cellulose and cellulase. *Cellulose* forms the polymers in cotton and linen. *Cellulase* is an enzyme used to prevent pilling and improve the texture and colour of cotton fabrics.

 Q2 *Describe **one** advantage of using cellulase to improve the finish of Tencel.*

2 marks

....

....

Acceptable answer

Cellulase is used to **stop the fibres fibrillating** therefore **reducing the pilling** that occurs on the surface of the fabric.

xaminer's Tip

Pilling refers to the small balls, which form at places where the fabric rubs against itself, e.g. inside of sleeves, side of blouse/jacket/jumper/cardigan.

You should be aware that:

☐ Products become obsolete.

☐ Different cultures influence textiles products.

OBSOLETE PRODUCTS

The fashion industry creates images for a short shelf life in order to create a new style or image the next season. This continuous process results in fashion items becoming obsolete very quickly; what is the height of fashion today is the item of clothing that you would definitely not wear in two years time!

There is a cycle in the fashion industry, which ensures the rise and decline of each fashion item. After a design has been seen on the catwalk it will be offered for sale in designer shops and may be worn and promoted by celebrities. This idea is then copied and sold at a much cheaper price in the High Street stores. It is then further simplified and sold in chain stores or supermarkets. At this point everyone is wearing the same design idea. Soon the market will tire of the product and the remaining stock will not sell. This stock might be sold in the sales but by now it is out of date and obsolete.

There are three ways in which products become obsolete:

- When something becomes old-fashioned and a new product is introduced with improved functional qualities.
- When the product wears out or breaks down, usually not too distant from the purchasing time and therefore does not fulfil its function. This is called planned obsolescence.
- When the product becomes old-fashioned in our minds, although it is still of good quality and performing well.

This is seen clearly in the textiles industry where jeans are marketed in an aggressive manner to create an 'artificial market'. The consumer is persuaded to buy the latest type of jeans, e.g. stretch jeans, decorated jeans or baggy jeans.

CULTURAL INFLUENCES ON TEXTILES

Designers take their ideas from a range of sources and these can include both cultural and historical contexts. Many textiles techniques date back hundreds, if not thousands, of years, e.g. tie-dye, batik, block and roller printing can all be traced back to Mexico and Peru as early as 1500 BC. By 500 AD batik, stencilling and tie-dye were used widely in Japan. Each culture put there own unique touch to the technique and used their own knowledge to influence the actual design ideas.

Block printing, which is two thousand years old, is still used extensively in Bangladesh today. A number of relief blocks are used to print different colours of intricate patterns, and the fabric created is used to produce tablecloths and other household products.

All aspects of the textiles market can be influenced by different cultures. Highly decorated jeans for example, are influenced by Indian embroideries found on Saris and hand-embroidered Chinese mandarin jackets. These embroidery techniques have also been used on expensive evening wear to enhance and embellish a range of items including jackets and dresses.

The decoration of fabric is influenced by many cultures. The use of batik techniques, dye colours and patterns can be seen in many textile products. These techniques are often adapted to suit improved technological equipment, thus ensuring fast production rather than the labour intensive hand-worked methods.

The patterns developed from different cultures are often adapted and used in commercial production in this country. Many soft furnishing fabrics are based on design ideas from across the world. Hieroglyphics for example, have been used to influence design and have often been used in borders and patterns on fabrics such as towels and household items. The ancient Egyptian patterns have been used extensively in fabric design and are often produced using a screen-printing method.

Examination questions

Q1   *Explain **one** reason why fashion items become obsolete so quickly.*

2 marks

....

....

Acceptable answer

Any one from:
- Fashion manufacturers need to **create a profit**, therefore **new designs are introduced making old designs obsolete**.
- An **artificial market** is created making the consumer think **they need to buy new fashion items**, thus **perfectly good products become obsolete**.

Q2   *Describe **one** way in which different cultures have influenced western fashion.*

2 marks

....

....

Acceptable answer

Any one from:
- **Batik, which originated in India**, has been used to **decorate fabrics** used for making dresses and skirts as well as men's shirts.
- Intricate **hand embroidery from China and India** has been adapted to **decorate clothing** such as jackets, jeans and evening wear, as well as items such as bags.

You need to know that:

☐ Manufacturing and consumers have a responsibility to the environment.

KEY POINTS

The production of textiles items has many impacts on the environment, from the use of natural resources to the waste that is generated. Manufacturing companies have begun to consider this problem and have taken steps to deal with the following range of issues.

ENERGY

Manufacturers must consider how much energy they are using in production processes and look for ways of reducing this consumption. The transportation of textiles products contributes to both energy use and emissions. All textile products need to be moved from the factory to the shop. They are usually transported by lorry or van. The use of a lorry or van means that petrol or diesel is being used. Petrol is produced from fossil fuels, which are a valuable resource that cannot be replaced. Fossil fuels are found deep down in the earth and have been created over thousands of years. They have to be recovered from the earth by drilling, in the case of oil and gas, and mining in the case of coal. As these sources of energy cannot be replaced it is important that we use them economically.

Wind and water power are alternative energy sources to fossil fuels and are renewable (can be replaced). Wind power has been developed in exposed areas across the country. Large propellers driven by the wind produce electricity. This electricity might be used to power textiles factories and machinery, for example. Although the use of alternative energy is encouraged, it is not always popular with the communities that live near the wind farms as some feel they are unsightly.

Companies are also reducing their consumption of mains water by drilling boreholes to draw their own water for use in cleaning fabrics. Sensors are being installed to machinery and lighting so they switch themselves off when they are not in use.

Emissions: These are not always visible but they can still damage the environment. Chemical gases from fabric finishes and fibre production are released into the atmosphere and can have a damaging effect on humans, plants and animals. Carbon dioxide is a colourless, odourless gas, which is dispersed into the atmosphere and contributes to global warming. It comes from the burning of fossil fuels. Emissions released into the atmosphere can be cleaned before they are released, and the use of computerised boilers can help with this process.

As well as using a valuable resource, lorries and vans also produce fumes which damage the environment. These fumes are called emissions and can have a damaging effect on humans, plants and animals. The carbon monoxide emissions from gases and from vehicles add to greenhouse gases, increasing the natural greenhouse effect and contributing to global warming. Many nations of the world have agreed to reduce the emissions generated over a set period of time. Currently, the UK has agreed to reduce its emissions to 12.5 per cent below the 1990 levels and reduce carbon monoxide levels to 20 per cent below the 1990 levels by 2010.

NATURAL RESOURCES

The use of natural resources can be conserved through the planting of managed forests. This means that for every tree cut down for use in production, another one is planted. In fact new trees are planted and are growing before established trees are cut down. The forests are managed to ensure that a supply of trees is always available. Trees are used in textiles production to make regenerated fibres. These fibres are made from wood pulp and are cellulose based. Tencel is produced from wood gathered from sustainable forests.

WASTE

The production of a textile product will also create other forms of waste. This can range from fabric remnants left over from production to paper and card waste from packaging. As much of this waste as possible must be recycled. It is important that companies are proactive at the beginning of the manufacturing process by considering the quantities of fabric and packaging required for a product and reviewing if it is possible to reduce the amount of resources that are being used. Products can be re-designed to avoid unnecessary waste, and the amount of packaging can be reduced where possible.

Recycling

Specialist companies will recycle waste products. Natural fabrics such as wool can be reduced back to fibres and these can be re-used. Only if a wool item contains a label 'pure new wool' has it actually been made from wool taken straight from the sheep. All wool products containing a label 'pure wool' have been recycled. Even every day items like plastic bottles can be recycled and used as fabric. Polartec fleece fabric has been developed from recycling plastic bottles. The plastic is reduced back to a molten state and reconstituted into a fibre.

Waste can be produced at various times during the production and use of a textiles item. As a result, there are a range of recycling processes and terms used for different stages of the textiles industry:

Pre-consumer textile waste

This is the result of the mill ends, clippings or goods damaged during production. Companies that grade pre-consumer textile waste are called rag sorters.

Post-consumer textile waste

Post-consumer textile waste is created from household waste such as bed linens, towels etc., or worn clothing. These are all collected and re-used or recycled. These items undergo a selective process of sorting, grading and separation into what is suitable for re-use or re-processing. Other items, which are recycled, can come under the category of 'vintage used clothing' – these are items that have come back into fashion and have monetary value.

Examination questions

Q1 *Explain **two** benefits to the environment of recycling within the fashion industry.*

....

....

....

....

Acceptable answer

Any one from:
* **Fibres can be obtained** from a recycled source, for example plastic bottles, therefore **reducing the waste** being dumped in landfill sites.
* Fabrics can be used from **old garments for patchwork or decoration** of garments, **thus reducing the amount of waste**.

Q2 *Give **three** ways textile manufacturers can reduce emissions.*

....

....

....

Acceptable answer

Any three from:
* cleaning emissions before release into the atmosphere
* reducing transportation
* reducing the application of chemical finishes
* reducing the production of synthetic fibres.

QUALITY ASSURANCE AND QUALITY CONTROL

You should be aware that:

☐ Textile manufacturing must set certain standards.

☐ Textiles products must be checked against these standards.

KEY POINTS

Every product produced, whether textiles or any other material, must meet certain standards. Before production begins a company will write down the standard of production and the quality of the product that must be reached. This is the **quality assurance**, i.e. the assurance to the customer that the specified quality has been reached. In order to guarantee this standard the textiles item is checked at critical points during production, this is **quality control**.

Before a production run, a number of prototype garments are made by the workforce so that the quality control department can assess the level of production. They will look for production problems that will affect the performance or function of the product. Very tiny faults, which will not be obvious to the customer, will be allowed through, e.g. interfacing slightly too small, facing of shirt slightly too big.

Every process has a set **tolerance level**. This is a minimum and maximum size allowance which the manufacturer has agreed at the beginning of production. Examples include: all seam widths are checked for consistent size; buttonholes should fit with the buttons; zips are correctly inserted; hems are even.

A company could check every product, but in batch and high volume production this is not realistic. Samples are checked throughout the working day and at different stages of the production line. Where a difficult construction technique is carried out there may be an automatic check, thus ensuring work is not passed through the system containing a fault. In the long run this reduces costs, as time is not wasted redoing substandard work.

Examination questions

Q1 When manufacturing a textiles product, quality assurance and quality control must be considered.

Explain what is meant by the terms:

a) *Quality assurance*

b) *Quality control*

4 marks

....

....

....

....

Acceptable answer

a) Quality assurance is the **standard written down before production begins** in order to decide the **quality of the processes and the finished product.**

b) Quality control is the **checking process** that takes place during production to check the **product meets the agreed standard.**

Q2 Give **two** quality control checks that must be made after a zip has been inserted into the centre back seam of a pinafore dress.

2 marks

....

....

Acceptable answer

Any two from:
- Centre back seam matches at the neck edge.
- Stitching is a suitable distance from teeth of zip.
- Stitching allows the slider to move up and down.
- Fabric covers the zip and meets in the middle of the zip.
- Stitching is straight.

Q3 *A jacket is fastened using buttons and buttonholes.*

*Give **two** quality control checks that the manufacturer must make during the production of the buttonholes.*

2 marks

....

....

Acceptable answer

Any two from:
- Stitching must be the correct size/tension (for the fabric).
- Satin stitch must be very close together (to prevent fraying).
- Buttonhole must be the correct length.
- Buttonhole must be cut straight.

Examiner's Advice

The text in brackets is not necessary to score the mark available for the answer given.

Section 4
Advice on design and product analysis questions

This section contains advice on how to answer:
- design questions (not short course)
- product analysis questions.

KEY POINTS

- The design questions on the foundation tier and higher tier will be different.
- The product analysis question for the full course will be the same on both foundation and higher tiers. It will appear as question 4 at foundation and question 1 at the higher level.
- The product analysis question for the short course will be the same on both foundation and higher tiers. It will appear as question 3 at foundation and question 1 at the higher level.
- Both the design question and the product analysis question will be divided into smaller part questions which use the same key words as listed in Section 1. The type of answers required also follow the same pattern as the examples given in Section 1.
- The way in which these two questions differ from others on the paper is that each will focus completely on a single product, that is, all 22 marks.
- The products used for each question will be different and will be introduced at the beginning of the question.
- Both questions will test your ability to apply knowledge and understanding, of the Specification content, to the identified product.

DESIGN QUESTIONS (NOT SHORT COURSE)

The design question will test your ability to produce two different, relevant and viable initial designs from a given specification. You must apply your knowledge and understanding gained from studying the following topics of Design and Technology: Textiles Technology to the production of your designs.

(a) Selection of materials and components:
- material form and intended manufacturing process
- functional properties of materials
- choice and fitness for purpose of materials and components.

(b) Processing and finishing materials:
- combination/processing of materials to create more useful properties
- functional properties of finishes – physical and visual.

(c) Manufacturing commercial products:
- manufacturing processes suited to the specified production volume.

(d) Design and market influence:
- environmental, moral and safety issues relating to material selection
- ease of manufacture of your design.

The following bullet points show the type of information given in each design question, supported by examples of wording. Each example is accompanied by brief explanations to help you identify the important things to consider and include in an answer. An example of a full design question with a model answer is included at the end of this section.

Each design question includes the following:
- A brief description of the background to the design situation. For example:
  'A manufacturer requires a small bag to be designed, to carry a mobile phone.'

- A list of specification points that your design ideas must satisfy. Each of these points will contain two linked elements, both of which must be satisfied in each of your designs to score full marks. An example of one specification point is:

  'Hold the mobile phone securely.'
- The two linked elements to be included in your design ideas are: 'Hold the mobile phone' and 'securely'.
- The instructions and marks available for each part of the question. For example:

 *Use notes and sketches to show **two** different designs of your product which meet the specification above* **(2 × 8 marks)**

Key words
'Use notes and sketches': your answer to the design question should be sketched and, where necessary, supported with notes that give descriptions and clarify the sketches by providing additional important information that cannot easily be shown by sketching.

 xaminer's Tip

You must look at the functional requirements of each specification point and present different methods by which those requirements are met in each of your two separate design ideas.

 xaminer's Tip

Remember, there can be many answers that all appear to be different for this type of question. However, all successful answers musts satisfy the common specification points given in the question.

 xaminer's Tip

In part 1 of the question, you should produce two different ideas to access both sets of 8 marks. This means your ideas must be technically different, not cosmetically different – that is, a different technical method by which the set design task is satisfied rather than just changing the colour or the shape. For example, the closing on the front of a fleece can be achieved by technically different methods, such as:
- a zip
- velcro

(b) *Three of the specification points are given below. Use these headings to evaluate **one** of your design ideas against the initial specification.* **(6 marks)**

xaminer's Tip

Remember the key word 'evaluate'. This means that one or two sentences are required where the suitability or value of your idea is judged. It can include both positive and negative points, with each point being linked to a feature of your design and being supported with a valid justification or reasoning.

xaminer's Tip

The evaluation you carry out here should result in your giving the examiner new/additional information relating to how well your design is likely to succeed or why it might fail or need further development. This new information will be contained in these judgements and their justification or reasoning. It will probably be in the form of an *explanation*; simply repeating information previously *described* in part **(a)** of your answer will not score marks here.

xaminer's Tip

Remember to divide the time you spend on this question in proportion to the marks available for each part, that is:

(a) design idea 1 **(8 marks)** – approximately 8 minutes
(b) design idea 2 **(8 marks)** – approximately 8 minutes
(c) evaluation **(6 marks)** – approximately 6 minutes.

Example design question

'A manufacturer requires a small bag to be designed to carry a mobile phone.'

The specification is that the product must:

- *hold the mobile phone securely*
- *be made of a durable fabric which will protect the phone*
- *be able to be attached to an item of clothing*
- *be easily produced as a one-off item.*

*In the spaces below use notes and sketches to show **two** ideas for the design of the product which meets this specification.* **(2 × 8 marks)**

Choose one of your design ideas and evaluate it against the three initial design specification points given below.

The product must hold the mobile phone securely.
The product must be made of a durable fabric which will protect the phone.
The product must be able to be attached to an item of clothing. **(6 marks)**

Model answer

DESIGN IDEA 1

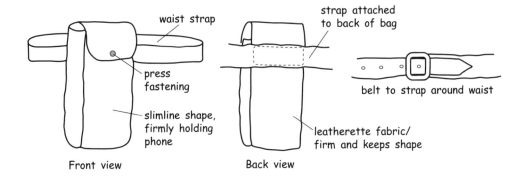

DESIGN IDEA 2

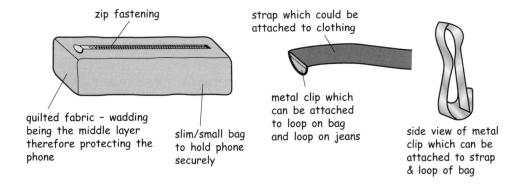

PRODUCT ANALYSIS QUESTIONS

Each product analysis question will give information about a commercially produced product in the form of:

- an illustration
- any additional data necessary for you to answer all part questions.

You will then be required to interpret this information and combine it with the knowledge and experience gained from studying Design and Technology: Textiles Technology to answer the part questions set from any of the following topics:

(a) Selection of materials and components:

- the working characteristics of materials in relation to their function within the product;
- the relationship of the material's final form in the product and the manufacturing process;
- functional properties of materials in relation to their use in the product;
- choice and fitness for purpose within the product of materials and components.

(b) Processing and finishing materials:

- combination or processing of materials to create more useful properties and how these have been used beneficially within the product;
- functional properties of finishes – physical and visual – and why they are important to the product;
- how the materials have been prepared for the manufacture of the product;
- how and why pre-manufactured standard components have been used in the product;
- where and/or why specified tolerances have been used in the manufacture of the product;
- how and/or why ICT has been used in the design and/or manufacture of the product.

(c) Manufacturing commercial products:

- an awareness of a manufacturing process suited to the specified production volume for the product and an understanding of why it is suitable
- an awareness of how ICT, including CAD/CAM, is used in batch or volume manufacture of the product.

(d) Design and market influence:

- evaluate the quality of design and quality of manufacture in terms of the product performance criteria related to the following – function, the needs and values of users, moral cultural and environmental considerations, the materials and processes used and safety;
- consider the design features that make the product suitable for manufacture in the specified quantity;
- planning of production for the product including production schedules, quality control and quality assurance.

(e) Give and justify points of specification for the given product.

xaminer's Tip

Remember, not all of these topics will be covered each year and just because a topic was covered in a previous year does not mean that it will not be included again.

Example questions
The following are examples of part question types that may be included in product analysis questions.

xaminer's Tip

Key words
Remember, the type and complexity of answers required for any part question is shown by the use of the key words used in the question, that is, Give, State, Name, Describe, Explain, etc.

For this example, the question would start by showing an illustration of a child's winter jacket designed for the five to eight age range. It would be labelled to show that it is quilted, has elasticated sleeves and is buttoned at the front.

Two points of specification for the jacket are:
- *it must keep the child warm*
- *it must keep the child dry.*

*Give **three** more points which must be included in the specification for the jacket. For each point give a reason why it must be included.*

a ....

Reason ....

b ....

Reason ....

c ....

Reason ....

(6 marks)

Acceptable answer

A full answer for 6 marks requires three valid points of specification for the product, each linked with a valid reason for its inclusion, for example:

a It should be easy to **put on/take off** and **do up/undo** because the **child should be able to do this**.

b It must **be lightweight** because **children cannot cope easily with heavy clothes**.

c It should be **tough and durable** because **children will give clothes rough use**.

xaminer's Tip

Note that each of the answers is given in two parts – the point of specification followed by the reason. The two parts are linked by the word 'because'.

Another key word may be used in this question – 'Complete'. For example:

 *After the fabric pieces have been cut to size from the templates, the jacket is to be volume produced using industrial methods. Complete the block diagram below to show **four** more main stages in the production process.*

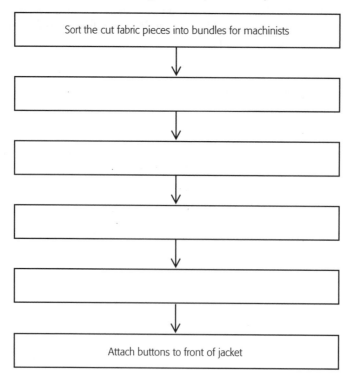

(5 marks)

Acceptable answer

A full answer for 5 marks requires four main stages to be written in the spaces provided, and in the correct sequence, for example four from: join shoulder seams – front and back to construct bodice; construct collar and attach to bodice; construct sleeves and attach to bodice; stitch through cuff and wasitband; complete casings at waist and buttonholes. You would receive 4 marks for the main stages and 1 mark for the correct sequence.

xaminer's Tip

Note that the wording of each stage in the question is a brief phrase. This is a guide to show the detail required in the answers; each stage of the answer given above is a brief phrase – single-word answers will seldom give enough information to fully identify an individual stage and earn the mark.